TRANSFORMATION
LETTING GOD MAKE A BETTER YOU

ALLAN MACHADO

Nampa, Idaho | www.pacificpress.com

Cover design: Christian Media Outlet
Cover design resources: GettyImages.com
Interior design: Aaron Troia

Copyright © 2024 by Pacific Press® Publishing Association
Printed in the United States of America
All rights reserved

The author assumes full responsibility for the accuracy of all facts and quotations as cited in this book.

Unless otherwise noted, Scripture is quoted from the New King James Version®. Copyright © 1982 by Thomas Nelson. Used by permission. All rights reserved.

Scripture quotations marked KJV are from the King James Version.

Scripture quotations marked NIV are from THE HOLY BIBLE, NEW INTERNATIONAL VERSION®. Copyright © 1973, 1978, 1984, 2011 by Biblica, Inc.® Used by permission. All rights reserved worldwide.

To order additional copies of this book, call toll-free 1-800-765-6955 or visit AdventistBookCenter.com.

ISBN 978-0-8163-6987-4

May 2024

Dedication

I dedicate this book
to all those who seek God with an earnest heart and want to grow in His ways,
to all who labor for the spiritual growth of others,
to all who hunger and thirst for Jesus and have set their minds to live close to God.

Contents

Introduction	7
Chapter 1: In Search of Real Transformation	9
Chapter 2: Transformation by Self-Awareness and Repentance	17
Chapter 3: Transformation by Confession and Forgiveness	27
Chapter 4: Transformation Through Relationship	35
Chapter 5: Transformation by Sanctification	47
Chapter 6: Transformation by Worship as a Lifestyle	53
Chapter 7: Transformation Is Conversion	61
Chapter 8: Transformation Through Bible Study	67
Chapter 9: Transformation Through Prayer	73
Chapter 10: Transformation Through Fasting	79
Chapter 11: Transformation Through Journaling	85
Chapter 12: Transformation Through Meditation	93
Chapter 13: Transformation Through Stewardship	99
Chapter 14: Transformation Through a Spiritual Retreat	107
Appendix: Spiritual Inventory	113

Introduction

For more than three decades, Jesus demonstrated in a real and practical way what man can be and do if he lives in constant communion with the Father. Following Jesus' example will mold and transform all who choose to follow Him. Jesus most commonly used the phrase *Son of Man* to refer to Himself. This phrase refers to the incomprehensible mystery that Christ, the anointed of God, who was "equal with God" (Philippians 2:5, 6), became "likeness of men" (verse 7), taking human nature. Our heavenly Father desires His children to be restored to the image of the invisible God made visible in the person of Jesus for the salvation of humanity.

To this end, *Transformation* was written to help you grow spiritually and solidify your relationship with Jesus.

In truth, when our lives are compared with the perfect life of Jesus Christ, we fall short because ever since sin entered this world, the human race has lived with the consequences of sin—sickness, gradual deterioration, and death. While most humans

Transformation

try to live a good life, our best efforts are not enough to overcome or atone for sin. However, Jesus was a completely righteousness, worthy, and just man. Only when we follow Jesus and allow His Spirit to work in our lives does real transformation happen. "We are to grow daily in spiritual loveliness. We shall fail often in our efforts to copy the divine pattern. We shall often have to bow down to weep at the feet of Jesus, because of our shortcomings and mistakes; but we are not to be discouraged."[1]

Many people wonder, *Can a human being be like Jesus? Is it really possible to be different? Can humans grow and mature spiritually so they may live in peace with God and their neighbors? If so, how?*

Transformation will help you grow in the basic concepts of the Word and intimacy with God. It is designed to be studied in small groups where you can develop a relationship of grace and growth in Christ that lasts a lifetime. Through these studies, you will recognize your need for Christ and know He is the only solution to living a life of joy and peace, hidden in the grace of God. To do this, you must follow Jesus, learn what He taught, and help others to come to know Jesus too. As you discover the satisfaction of following Christ and enjoying a relationship with Him, your relationship with Jesus will become increasingly real and practical, and you will see Him in every aspect of your daily life.

Living for Jesus means that you have developed a personal relationship in which you recognize Jesus Christ as your Lord and Savior forever. This relationship will transform your character, replace your values with the values of the kingdom of God, and make you part of Christ's mission in your home, the church, and the world.

---

1. Ellen G. White, *Selected Messages*, bk. 1 (Washington, DC: Review and Herald®, 1958), 337.

Chapter 1

In Search of Real Transformation

A my Carmichael, a Christian missionary to India, made the following observation about spiritual growth:

> Sometimes when we read the words of those who have been more than conquerors, we feel almost despondent. I feel that I shall never be like that. But they won through step by step, by little bits of wills, little denials of self, little inward victories, by faithfulness in very little things. They became what they are. No one sees these little hidden steps. They only see the accomplishment, but even so, those small steps were taken. There is no sudden triumph, no spiritual maturity that is the work of the moment.

So persistence is a key to spiritual growth. Similarly, an athlete on a running tour of his country had to overcome several obstacles: heat, cold, rain, and sun. When he reached the end, he was

Transformation

interviewed: "What was the biggest challenge you had to face?" He replied, "My biggest obstacles were the little pebbles that got into my sneakers."

Winning the smallest battles can often be the most difficult. After all, it's the little things that infiltrate your entire life (1 Corinthians 5:6). Every day, you find yourself with the dilemma of following your desires or fulfilling the will of God. It is a matter of choice. God wants you to conform to His will so all goes well for you (Deuteronomy 4:40). How can you achieve this? When you ponder how to discover the will of God for your life, you may ask yourself where to start. Usually, it comes down to insignificant desires, small inclinations, small rejections impacting the ego, victories of faith in small things. You might think you cannot fathom what God thinks or understand what He has designed for your life. Nevertheless, God wants to teach you how He reveals His will and how you can fulfill it.

Choosing to fulfill the will of God characterized the life of Christ. His purpose was to glorify God and do His will, even in the most insignificant details of life (Luke 22:42; John 5:30; 6:38). While Jesus was on Earth, He fulfilled the will of God. Would a person deliberately wish to traverse moments of humiliation, anguish, and death? If Jesus had sought His own benefit, would He have chosen the rejection and humiliation He suffered? Jesus experienced such things because they were part of the will of His Father as well as part of an eternal plan that He had designed before the foundation of the world (1 Peter 1:20).

Jesus' purpose while He was in the flesh is revealed in Hebrews 5:7–9: "Who, in the days of His flesh, when He had offered up prayers and supplications, with vehement cries and tears to Him who was able to save Him from death, and was heard because of His godly fear, though He was a Son, yet He learned obedience by the things which He suffered. And having been perfected, He became

In Search of Real Transformation

the author of eternal salvation to all who obey Him." "Having been perfected" can best be understood as "having achieved the stature of complete maturity."[1] The word used here to describe Christ's perfection is *teleioō* in Greek, suggesting the idea of having finished the task. Christ accomplished what He had set Himself to achieve because He had demonstrated His obedience unto death and was perfected through the fulfillment of the purpose of God and His will.

Jesus' obedience is demonstrated when, after the Last Supper and before the crucifixion, He prayed in Gethsemane, "Father, if it is Your will, take this cup away from Me; nevertheless not My will, but Yours, be done" (Luke 22:42). Just as Christ fully submitted to the will of God, Christians discover that the secret to success relies exclusively on developing a spirit of obedience and reverent fear so that they, too, can say, "Father . . . not my will but Yours be done." This reliance is achieved step by step as Christians learn to listen to God and understand His purpose. Taking small steps of faith will prepare you for the decisive hour when you have to completely surrender your will to the will of God.

Real transformation is a journey that will lead you through prayer, suffering, tears, and spiritual defeats to a Gethsemane where you will have to finally surrender in obedience to your personal Savior. Only when you understand what it means to say "not my will, but Yours be done" will you be glorified in the same way Jesus was glorified.

The word used in Greek to describe this kind of transformation is *metamorphoō*, from which comes the English word *metamorphosis*. Just as animals change and transform through the process known as metamorphosis, the process of spiritual growth touches every aspect of a person's life. The person is gradually transformed into a citizen of the kingdom of heaven through the work of Christ.

Transformation

Metamorphosis is a biological process by which many insects, amphibians, mollusks, crustaceans, echinoderms, and tunicates develop from birth to maturity by means of large and abrupt structural and physiological changes. This process is usually accompanied by changes in habitat and behavior. One of the most interesting processes of transformation is that of butterflies:

1. The butterfly starts its life in an egg, which is placed in a host plant that will sustain it with food.
2. The caterpillar leaves the egg, feeds, and changes its skin to fool its predators.
3. Inside the chrysalis, the pupa's cells dissolve until it becomes a winged being.
4. After a long process, the chrysalis opens to reveal an adult butterfly.

Like the butterfly, the Christian needs to experience a metamorphosis. Mere knowledge of the gospel or intellectual acceptance of the grace of God does not constitute what God expects of us. It is only the beginning. Accepting grace goes beyond an intellectual statement. It is unquestionably reflected in the practical life of the believer—the transformation is inevitable. No one who knows Jesus is left the same. No one who accepts the grace of God continues to live in rebellion against God. The mind and the heart of the believer must be transformed.

But how? How does a Christian experience this metamorphosis? When a person understands the sacrifice of Jesus on the cross of Calvary and meditates on His divine grace—an undeserved gift—the Christian can arrive at only one conclusion: I must present myself as a living sacrifice, holy and pleasing to God (Romans 12:1). If Jesus died for me, the least I can do is to live for Him. The inexplicable gift of the Son of God demands my

In Search of Real Transformation

heart, my mind, my whole life. As a Christian, I no longer need to come to God with sacrificial animals, as in Old Testament times, but with the living sacrifice of a life wholly committed to my Savior, I offer my holy life, pleasing to God.

The Bible explains that Christ desires that we be transformed to the measure of the fullness of the stature of Christ and adds that "we should no longer be children, tossed to and fro . . . , but, speaking the truth in love, may grow up in all things" (Ephesians 4:11–16). The Word exhorts Christians not to conform to this world (Romans 12:2). In other words, do not allow yourself to be molded to the patterns of the world. The world represents society or the system that man has created as he searches for his own happiness away from God. It is a kingdom antagonistic to the kingdom of God. The word used in the Bible is *suschēmatizō*, which means conformed to another's pattern. When you come to the kingdom of God, you must abandon the schemes, the patterns of thoughts, and the lifestyles of the world. The Bible expresses this concept as follows:

> I beseech you therefore, brethren, by the mercies of God, that you present your bodies a living sacrifice, holy, acceptable to God, which is your reasonable service (Romans 12:1).

> He gave me the priestly duty of proclaiming the gospel of God, so that the Gentiles might become an offering acceptable to God, sanctified by the Holy Spirit (Romans 15:16, NIV).

> Therefore by Him let us continually offer the sacrifice of praise to God, that is, the fruit of our lips, giving thanks to His name (Hebrews 13:15).

Transformation

> But do not forget to do good and to share, for with such sacrifices God is well pleased (verse 16).

> And do not be conformed to this world, but be transformed by the renewing of your mind, that you may prove what is that good and acceptable and perfect will of God (Romans 12:2).

In addition to not letting yourself be conformed to the world, you must be transformed by means of the renewal of your mind, which means you should think the way God thinks as the knowledge of God is revealed in your life through His Word. Only then can you experience His direct leading in your life. And, as you know Him more and learn to love and trust Him, you will realize His ways are not burdensome. His will is good, acceptable, and perfect.

Here are three steps to follow as you seek the will of God based on Romans 12:1, 2:

1. Present yourself as a living sacrifice, holy and acceptable to the Lord.
2. Detoxify from the things of this world.
3. Experience a metamorphosis through the renewing of your mind.

Jesus invites His followers to seek an intimate relationship with God so they could grow spiritually. This spiritual growth is not based on religious rites or ceremonies; rather, it is a gift that is gained through grace. The development of a passionate relationship with God goes further than practicing spiritual disciplines, even though these are an excellent start. Therefore, spirituality is not merely about morality, good conduct, living

In Search of Real Transformation

a sinless life (perfectionism), or a pious life with holy verbal or corporal language. It is not only about doctrinal purity, biblical knowledge, or spiritual disciplines. Neither does it have to do with membership, church positions, or lifestyle choices such as diet, dress, and exercise. It's not necessarily manifested in signs and wonders, speaking in tongues, or performing miracles. It bears no connection to a sanguine temperament or a certain level of friendliness or generosity. Neither does it have to do with seriousness, marital status, age, gender, or race.

Instead, as Ellen G. White expresses: "Constantly we must submit our will to God's will, our way to God's way. Our peculiar ideas will strive constantly for the supremacy, but we must make God all and in all. We are not free from the failings of humanity, but we must constantly strive to be free from these failings, not to be perfect in our own eyes, but perfect in every good work."[2]

Then, the Bible says, "For it is God who works in you both to will and to do for His good pleasure" (Philippians 2:13). "Not that I have already attained, or am already perfected; but I press on, that I may lay hold of that for which Christ Jesus has also laid hold of me. Brethren, I do not count myself to have apprehended; but one thing I do, forgetting those things which are behind and reaching forward to those things which are ahead, I press toward the goal for the prize of the upward call of God in Christ Jesus" (Philippians 3:12–14).

In conclusion, when thinking about spiritual transformation, keep these concepts in mind:

- Transformation is necessary for a true disciple of Christ.
- Transformation is primarily a process, not an event.
- Transformation is the work of God in you as a believer but requires your presence in the process.
- Transformation involves practical experiences that will

Transformation

help you live out an intimate relationship with Christ, walking and living as Christ would.
- Transformation is not a process that develops as only one part of your life. God is interested in not only your spiritual life but also your whole life.
- Transformation can happen at any time and in any place. It is not restricted by human laws and practices.
- Transformation is not individualistic. It can take place in community and finds expression in service to others.
- Transformation is not determined by temperament or specific situations in life. At this very moment, it's within reach of anyone who desires it.

You cannot measure transformation. Instead, spiritual transformation is fueled by a growing ability to love God and others. External and superficial indexes cannot evaluate it. The ideal is always greater. The goal is unattainable. But in Christ, transformation is possible.

Reflection
Are you willing to submit your will to the will of God? What does this mean? How can you, in a practical way, present yourself as a pleasing offering to God?

---

1. Francis D. Nichol, ed., *The Seventh-day Adventist Bible Commentary*, vol. 7 (Washington, DC: Review and Herald®, 1980), 430.
2. Ellen G. White, *The Upward Look* (Washington, DC: Review and Herald®, 1982), 218.

Chapter 2

Transformation by Self-Awareness and Repentance

The Bible teaches that through disobedience, sin entered the world and, through sin, death (Romans 5:12). In more practical terms, the Hebrew words used to define sin refer to rebellion against God, evil intent, disloyalty, and vanity. Here are some of the Hebrew words and definitions for sin that we should keep in mind:

- *Khata'*—to sin, err, miss the mark, incur guilt (Exodus 9:27).
- *Pesha'*—rebellion or transgression (Psalm 51:3).
- *'Aon*—perversity, depravity, iniquity (Isaiah 53:6, 11).
- *Ma'al*—an unfaithful or treacherous act against man or against God (Ezekiel 15:8).
- *'Aven*—vanity, iniquity, wickedness, trouble, affliction (Psalm 10:7).

The Judeo-Christian tradition, whose fundamental source is

Transformation

the Bible, has understood sin, in general terms, as the estrangement of man from the will of God. In agreement with the Old Testament, the will of God is represented by the Law, precepts, and statutes given by God to the children of Israel and recorded in the sacred books.

The still prevailing religious concept of sin as a "moral crime" refers to the voluntary or involuntary transgression of norms or religious regulations. Since there are innumerable standards of this type, countless sins are assigned greater, lesser, or no punishment according to different beliefs. In Judges 20:16, the word used to refer to the Benjamites as those who "could sling a stone at a hair's breadth and not miss" is *khata'* (see also Job 5:24). It also applies to deviating from moral goals, such as in Proverbs 8:36 which says that he who finds pious wisdom finds life, but "he who sins [*khata'*] against me [God] wrongs his own soul."

Regardless of how we assign significance to voluntary or involuntary transgressions, one of the cardinal truths we find in the Bible is that, since the Fall, humanity has been naturally inclined to "miss the target." In other words, human nature is sinful and destitute of God's grace, even when we are trying to be righteous. The Bible describes the reality of human sinful nature:

> But we are all like an unclean thing,
> And all our righteousnesses are like filthy rags;
> We all fade as a leaf,
> And our iniquities, like the wind,
> Have taken us away (Isaiah 64:6).

In this sense, *sinful nature* refers to who we are and is unrelated to what we do. In describing this state, Ellen G. White puts it this way, "No deep-seated love for Jesus can dwell in the heart that does not realize its own sinfulness."[1]

Transformation by Self-Awareness and Repentance

When we develop this awareness of who we are, separate from our good or bad behaviors, we will be able to appreciate more the salvation provided by Jesus as He gave His life at Calvary. Then, and only then, we will understand that no man will ever be able to say, "I deserve salvation." One of the purposes of the plan of salvation is to show, throughout eternity, the ever-deepening riches of the grace of God. Thus, there is no reason why anyone would boast (see Ephesians 2:8, 9).

Ellen G. White expands on this truth: "Let no one take the limited, narrow position that any of the works of man can help in the least possible way to liquidate the debt of his transgression. This is a fatal deception. . . . This matter is so dimly comprehended that thousands upon thousands claiming to be sons of God are children of the wicked one, because they will depend on their own works."[2] "He who is trying to reach heaven by his own works in keeping the law, is attempting an impossibility."[3]

This idea is behind a story about a time when the King of Prussia, Frederick the Great, visited a Berlin jail. All but one of the prisoners fell on their knees, asking to be pardoned for their crimes because they were innocent. The one remained standing in silence. Frederick called him and asked, "Why are you here?"

"Armed robbery, your majesty," the man replied.

"Are you guilty?" asked Frederick.

"Yes, your Majesty; I deserve the punishment," was his answer.

Frederick called the jailer and ordered him to release the robber, telling him: "Quickly, release this culprit; I cannot allow him to continue in this prison where he can corrupt so many innocent people who are here unjustly."

Recognizing your need is the first step, which brings you closer to Jesus. As long as you deny the reality of your sinful nature, think you are in control, make excuses for the stains that tarnish your character, and think you do not need forgiveness, Jesus

Transformation

will have no meaning for you. The Bible teaches that we are all sinners and, therefore, condemned to suffer the consequences of sin. All men, without exception, are full of weaknesses and flaws. However, the Christian paradox is that times of weakness can be transformed into occasions for strength (2 Corinthians 12:9, 10). Defeat can always turn into victory. True strength of character comes from weakness, distrust of self, and surrender to the will of God. He who is strong in his own strength trusts himself rather than depending on God and often does not realize his need for divine grace.

"Can we possibly be saved?" was the desperate cry of the prophet Isaiah. Will there be hope for the sinful man? Paul answers the question that man has been asking since the world was born: "I do not set aside the grace of God" (Galatians 2:21). The understanding that you are sinful and hopelessly condemned to death is the biblical truth that opens the door to divine grace and a relationship with God. Understanding that sinners deserve the wrath of God and that they receive grace through Jesus is the best news a sinner can receive. When the Christian finally understands this, his life is full of hope. To the darkness of his sinful reality, the light of the grace of God arrives. God invites us,

> "Come now, and let us reason together,"
> Says the LORD,
> "Though your sins are like scarlet,
> They shall be as white as snow;
> Though they are red like crimson,
> They shall be as wool" (Isaiah 1:18).

The great heroes of the Bible, such as Noah, Abraham, Moses, Elijah, and Daniel, all understood this important concept: only those who have found the face of God in need and have felt Him

Transformation by Self-Awareness and Repentance

close when they experience difficult times and afflictions know what it really means to depend on the Creator. They have tasted the power and grace of God. He who has never seen the glory of the Lord in the midst of suffering has missed the deepest joy of this earthly life. As Paul said, "I have been crucified with Christ; it is no longer I who live, but Christ lives in me; and the life which I now live in the flesh I live by faith in the Son of God, who loved me and gave Himself for me" (Galatians 2:20, 21).

Reflecting upon my need for God's grace, I wrote this personal prayer:

> All my hopes I have placed on my Jesus.
> All my pleasures in Him I have placed.
> And because of this, life has been glorious—
> Just as glorious for me was His death.
> Pure of heart, as you lift up your prayer
> With a humble and penitent soul,
> Find in Jesus your peace, find your pleasure,
> And let Him turn your pain into joy.
> I have tasted the pain this world offers
> And then lost my soul's bliss;
> Like a bottomless spring was my weeping
> From the pain that I suffered and grieved.
> But then I turned my eyes upon Jesus,
> Filled with love and compassion serene,
> And my soul was immediately gladdened,
> For in Him I've found solace and peace.

The Bible teaches that repentance is the only, but inescapable, condition of God's forgiveness and restoration of His favor. Divine forgiveness and favor are never denied to the genuinely repentant person. Repentance is the beginning of a true relationship with God.

Transformation

Concerning repentance, G. F. Moore writes: "The Mishnah [oral rabbinic teachings] . . . makes repentance the indispensable condition of the remission of every kind of sin, and this, with the other side of it, namely, that God freely and fully remits the sins of the penitent, is a cardinal doctrine of Judaism; it may properly be called the Jewish doctrine of salvation."[4] "Repentance is the sole, but inexorable, condition of God's forgiveness and the restoration of his favor, and the divine forgiveness and favor are never refused to genuine repentance."[5] Then, he adds,

> The pre-eminence of repentance is expressed in the following passage: "Men asked Wisdom, What is the doom of the sinner? It answered, 'Evil pursues sinners' (Prov. 13, 21); they asked Prophecy the same question, and it answered, 'The soul (the individual) that sins shall die' (Ezekiel 18, 4); they asked the Law, and it answered, 'Let him bring a trespass offering (*asham*) and it shall be forgiven him.' . . . They asked the Holy One, blessed is He, and he answered, 'Let him repent, and it shall be forgiven him.' This is the meaning of the text, 'Good and right is the Lord, therefore will he instruct sinners in the way' (Psalm 25, 8)." That is, he shows them the way that they may repent.[6]

Sin has anesthetized our consciences to the point that we do not know how to relate to God. This condition of man is described thus: "There seems to be a cloudy atmosphere that has gathered about the soul of man and that has shut in the mind. It is next to impossible to break through this atmosphere of doubt and unbelief. It is next to impossible to arouse his vital interests so that he may understand what he must do to be saved."[7] The deception of sin has become a science in this

Transformation by Self-Awareness and Repentance

world. Evil has been able to control human interests in such a way that they reflect the malevolent image of their author. The image of holiness, of benevolence and love originally placed in the human being, has been almost totally obliterated, obscured, and destroyed.

The common Hebrew word used for repentance is interesting. The word is *shub*, which means "to turn back." Repentance is turning in the opposite direction from evil and moving toward God. Time after time, the Bible speaks of this turn from evil toward God (see Ezekiel 33:11; Jeremiah 31:18, 19; and Hosea 14:1, 2). The message of repentance has always been expressed in terms of hope and trust for the repentant sinner. Repentance is always accessible. There may be moments in which you wonder whether the doors of heaven are closed to your prayers because you don't receive the answer you desire, but never wonder whether the doors to repentance are closed to you. There may be repentance as long as there is life. The hand of God stretches to take the hand of the penitent and save him from the wrath of justice. As Martin Luther is credited with saying, "Between the mud and the mount, thy mercy I sought, and thy mercy I found." No one has walked so far that he cannot repent and turn to God. Let no man say, "Because I have sinned, there is no hope for me," but trust in God and repent, and God will receive him.

Repentance is truly at the center of Christian faith. It's the foundation of spiritual growth. Jesus' message of repentance was the same that was taught by the prophets of the Old Testament and John the Baptist. Nevertheless, it becomes imperative that we know the difference between repentance and remorse. In the Bible, these are two very different words, even if they look like they mean the same. For example, when the Bible speaks of Judas's repentance in Matthew 27:3, the word used is

Transformation

metamelomai, which means "regret." Judas returned to give back the thirty silver coins because he felt remorse. As a result, he hung himself because he did not have the courage to recognize his sin and repent of it. His proud heart did not allow him to seek God's forgiveness.

On the other hand, the word *metanoia*, translated as "repentance," has a completely different meaning from *remorse*; rather, it means "a change of mind," or a reformation (Luke 5:32). This concept is what the Bible refers to when speaking of the repentance of David and Peter, both of whom recognized their sin, wept bitterly, repented, and were restored because of their sincere repentance.

A heart of repentance is reflected in a very beautiful prayer that followers of Judaism say three times a day: "Return us, our Father, to Your Torah and draw us near, our Sovereign, to Your service, and bring us back to complete repentance before You. Blessed are You Adonai, Who welcomes repentance."[8]

When Jesus calls you to repentance, He is calling you to turn away from sin, to a complete surrender, to true confession, and to a total change of direction. And Jesus says, "The doors are always open for those who repent."

Reflection

What is repentance? How has divine grace changed your life? Is there a sin you have regretted (*metamelomai*) but not yet repented (*metanoia*) of? What would it take for you to experience sincere repentance?

---

1. Ellen G. White, *Steps to Christ* (Washington, DC: Review and Herald®, 1977), 65.

2. Ellen G. White, *Selected Messages*, bk. 1 (Washington, DC: Review and Herald®, 1958), 343.

3. White, 364.

Transformation by Self-Awareness and Repentance

4. George Foot Moore, *Judaism in the First Centuries of the Christian Era*, vol. 1 (Cambridge: Harvard University Press, 1927), 500.

5. Moore, 520.

6. Moore, 533.

7. Ellen G. White, *Faith and Works* (Nashville, TN: Southern Publishing Association, 1979), 64.

8. "The Amidah Prayer (part 1)," *Jewish Education by Design,* accessed December 13, 2023, https://jebd.org.il/resource/the-amidah-prayer-part-one/.

Chapter 3

Transformation by Confession and Forgiveness

The Bible teaches that, to develop an intimate relationship with God, it is necessary to confess our sins and seek Him with an attitude of repentance. Many Christians have a problem understanding the concept of sin. It is difficult to accept that, even when you try to be good, there are areas in your life that remain a constant test. You may harbor lust, envy, egocentrism, or dishonesty or make hurtful comments to others. Although it is difficult and cumbersome to accept our mistakes, it may be even more difficult to confess them, even privately, in prayer to God. However, that is clearly what God requires. "If we confess our sins, He is faithful and just to forgive us our sins and to cleanse us from all unrighteousness" (1 John 1:9).

The confession of sin, by itself, is not all that God requires. He asks you to repent, to give up your sinful ways and, instead, learn to walk with Him. The Bible declares that Jesus intercedes for you before the heavenly Father and is willing to forgive you when you confess your offenses.

Transformation

> As you see the enormity of sin, as you see yourself as you really are, do not give up to despair. It was sinners that Christ came to save. We have not to reconcile God to us, but—O wondrous love!—God in Christ is "reconciling the world unto Himself." 2 Corinthians 5:19. He is wooing by His tender love the hearts of His erring children. . . .
>
> When Satan comes to tell you that you are a great sinner, look up to your Redeemer and talk of His merits. That which will help you is to look to His light. Acknowledge your sin, but tell the enemy that "Christ Jesus came into the world to save sinners" and that you may be saved by His matchless love. 1 Timothy 1:15.[1]

True confession of sin manifests itself in two dimensions. The first has to do with God. King David expresses that while he hid his sin and did not confess it, his bones grew old (Psalm 32:3). But when he confessed his sin, he felt joy and gladness, and his broken bones rejoiced (Psalm 51:8). Confession is the medicine that heals the pain of the soul and opens the door to the forgiveness of God. Man finds peace and relief when he opens his heart to God with a spirit of confession and repentance. "My little children, these things I write to you, so that you may not sin. And if anyone sins, we have an Advocate with the Father, Jesus Christ the righteous" (1 John 2:1, 2).

God wants to create a new heart and a righteous spirit within you. One of the most beautiful promises of the Bible appears is contained in a confession: God never removes His Holy Spirit from you, and He returns to you the joy of salvation. Confession also manifests itself in another dimension. People must not only confess their sins to God but also confess to and ask forgiveness from their neighbors. When we hurt our neighbors, we must

Transformation by Confession and Forgiveness

recognize it and ask for forgiveness. This is not only approved by Heaven but also provides healing to those involved. Confessing your faults heals your soul and also the spirit of the person who was hurt.

I am reminded of a story of a pastor who, at the end of his sermon, asked the congregation a question to confirm that the message had been understood: "Can someone tell me what we must do before we can obtain forgiveness for our sins?" Absolute silence reigned throughout the congregation. After a moment, a child shouted from the end of the room, "We have to sin!" I suspect no one has any problem meeting this requirement. But the Word reveals that there is another prerequisite for experiencing the forgiveness of God in your life. This prerequisite is that you have the resolve to confess your faults, to be purified and washed with celestial hyssop.

Confession includes recognizing sin specifically, keeping no hidden sin and being conscious of your weaknesses and tendencies, genuinely confessing sin, asking for forgiveness and mercy, and receiving forgiveness from God. Satan seeks to enslave us, reminding us of the errors of the past. God wants to free us from guilt. "Confess your trespasses to one another, and pray for one another, that you may be healed. The effective, fervent prayer of a righteous man avails much" (James 5:16).

The Bible teaches that, to develop an intimate relationship with God, it is necessary to ask for forgiveness and learn to forgive.

"I had a brother and I betrayed him." With these words, African writer Laurens van der Post begins his book entitled *The Seed and the Sower*.[2] The book recounts the story of two brothers who lived in a small village in southern Africa. The older brother was tall, athletic, a good student, and a natural leader. His younger brother was different. He had a deformed spinal cord and struggled to make his way in life with his physical defects. However, he

Transformation

had the gift of a sweet and melodious voice. He sang. He liked to sing and did so wonderfully. The two brothers went to the same private school outside their home village.

One night, some of the older brother's friends cornered the young man and, ripping his shirt, began mocking and laughing at his physical defect, at the same time demanding that he sing. The young man was completely destroyed, humiliated, and full of rancor. The older brother knew what he was going through but did nothing to defend his brother. The young man survived the embarrassment but was left with a broken spirit. He returned to his family's ranch in the village to live his life in sadness and seclusion. The story recounts that he never sang again.

Many years later, the older brother had a dream that tormented him and would not leave him in peace. "I have to return, to ask my brother forgiveness for what I did to him. He hoped that I would defend him; however, to keep my popularity with my group of young friends, I betrayed him." He returned and apologized to his brother. They shared a teary embrace, and the brother forgave him. "I knew," the older brother said, "that he had forgiven me, when at dawn, when it was still dark, I heard a melodious song. It was my brother, singing a song that we would sing when we were boys. The melody flowed from a heart that had finally found the freedom offered by forgiveness." The younger brother had to make a decision when his brother asked him for forgiveness. He could forgive him or simply continue his life of pain, open wounds, resentment, and hate.

How difficult is it to forgive our debtors? How difficult does it become to forgive those who hurt you, who fill your life with sadness, abuse, contempt, and bitterness? The saddest thing is to notice that you are going through life repeating the same pattern. Studies show that children of shattered marriages tend to also end their marriages. Children of abusive and impatient parents end up

Transformation by Confession and Forgiveness

being abusers and impatient themselves. Betrayal is repaid with betrayal, humiliation with humiliation. And so, you fill yourself with bad feelings that take away your peace and joy. And without realizing it, you become a debtor to the same debts that you have not forgiven.

Consider the following questions: Who is the captive of resentment and pain in that prison of vengeance, hate, and bitterness when no forgiveness is offered? Whose life is destroyed, and which soul withers and dries? Whose mind is captive, and who is the one left with numbed emotions? If the young man had decided to cling to the pain of resentment and the desire for revenge, he would have won only more pain, more resentment, and more desire for revenge. Holding on to the bitterness of past wounds locks you in your own prison of resentment. You may have simply learned to survive with your wounds and bitterness. In many cases, you know you are not to blame for the pain you carry inside. It could have happened when you were young. These are wounds that were inflicted by people who should have loved and protected you. These were incidents that, beyond the physical damage, hurt your soul and made you feel shame, contempt, and emptiness.

Let us meditate on this topic in the light of the parable of the debtor recorded by Matthew. Here is the question Peter asks Jesus, prompting the explanation in the form of a parable: "Lord, how many times shall I forgive my brother or sister who sins against me? Up to seven times?" (Matthew 18:21, NIV).

> Jesus answered, "I tell you, not seven times, but seventy-seven times.
>
> "Therefore, the kingdom of heaven is like a king who wanted to settle accounts with his servants. As he began the settlement, a man who owed him ten

Transformation

thousand bags of gold was brought to him. Since he was not able to pay, the master ordered that he and his wife and his children and all that he had be sold to repay the debt.

"At this the servant fell on his knees before him. 'Be patient with me,' he begged, 'and I will pay back everything.' The servant's master took pity on him, canceled the debt and let him go.

"But when that servant went out, he found one of his fellow servants who owed him a hundred silver coins. He grabbed him and began to choke him. 'Pay back what you owe me!' he demanded.

"His fellow servant fell to his knees and begged him, 'Be patient with me, and I will pay it back.'

"But he refused. Instead, he went off and had the man thrown into prison until he could pay the debt. When the other servants saw what had happened, they were outraged and went and told their master everything that had happened.

"Then the master called the servant in. 'You wicked servant,' he said, 'I canceled all that debt of yours because you begged me to. Shouldn't you have had mercy on your fellow servant just as I had on you?' In anger his master handed him over to the jailers to be tortured, until he should pay back all he owed.

"This is how my heavenly Father will treat each of you unless you forgive your brother or sister from your heart" (verses 22–35, NIV).

Modern scholars offer a better understanding of the narrative by calculating the debt value in silver in Jesus' times. "Ten thousand bags" or "talents" (NKJV) would be equivalent to about

Transformation by Confession and Forgiveness

200,000 years of wags for a day laborer. And, "one hundred silver coins" or "denarii" was "the ordinary pay for a 100 days of work."[3] This begs the question: Which debt sent the first debtor to jail again? Was it the debt he had with the king or the debt someone had with him? What enslaved this debtor was not his tremendous debt to the king but his inability to forgive the relatively small debt someone owed him. He who refuses to forgive others denies himself the blessing of being forgiven as well. His sin is always before him.

Leave resentment behind, and put the remission of your sins in the hands of God. Let's look at Calvary for a moment and remember the words of Jesus when He hung on the cross: "Father, forgive them, for they do not know what they do" (Luke 23:34). We cannot question the reality of the pain caused by the injuries and injustice He experienced. He was not paying His own debt because He was innocent. Yet He said, "Father, forgive them.

Beloved, Jesus does not doubt your sorrows. He does not deny the reality of the injustice in your life. He does not ignore that your wounds often bleed or that you bear the burden of the sins of others. He does not deny the reality that you carry burdens in your life even though you are innocent. For Him, the important thing is not the pain and suffering. For Jesus, the important thing is healing for your soul.

What must you do to be released from the burdens that destroy your existence and wither your bones? The answer is difficult to accept, but it's the medicine your soul needs: You must forgive. Paul counsels, "Beloved, do not avenge yourselves, but rather give place to wrath; for it is written, 'Vengeance is Mine, I will repay,' says the Lord" (Romans 12:19). And Jesus taught His followers to pray the following: "And forgive us our debts, as we forgive our debtors." (Matthew 6:12). Then He continued, "For if you forgive men their trespasses, your heavenly Father will also forgive

Transformation

you. But if you do not forgive men their trespasses, neither will your Father forgive your trespasses" (verses 14, 15).

True spiritual transformation requires that we learn to forgive. True forgiveness is a decision made consciously, not emotionally. It is offered; it does not wait for a request. It casts out resentment and makes you free. Do not expect to heal or forget before you forgive. In forgiving, you consciously choose not to allow the past to dictate your life in the present and future. You will no longer be a product of your past; you will be a new creature in Christ. You will be able to evaluate your past in the light of the redeeming work of Christ. You will enjoy God's forgiveness. Forgiving the person who hurt you does not make him or her good, but it frees you from the weight you carry inside.

Reflection

Who and what do you need to forgive to enjoy the forgiveness of God in your life?

---

1. Ellen G. White, *Steps to Christ* (Washington, DC: Review and Herald®, 1977), 35, 36.

2. Laurens Van der Post, *The Seed and the Sower* (London: Hogarth Press, 1963)

3. Blue Letter Bible, s.v. "denarion," accessed Deember 18, 2023, https://www.blueletterbible.org/lexicon/g1220/kjv/tr/0-1/; Blue Letter Bible, s.v. "denarius," accessed May 1, 2024, https://www.blueletterbible.org/search/Dictionary/viewTopic.cfm?topic=IT0002641

Chapter 4

Transformation Through Relationship

The Bible teaches that salvation is a gift that comes from God, one that man accepts by faith in the perfect sacrifice of Christ. Even so, salvation for sinners seems impossible. However, when the disciples asked Jesus, "Who then can be saved?" He answered, "With men this is impossible, but with God all things are possible" (Matthew 19:25, 26). Shortly before Jesus' redemptive death, in His prayer to the Father for His disciples, Christ expressed in precise words the plan for salvation: "And this is eternal life, that they may know You, the only true God, and Jesus Christ whom You have sent" (John 17:3). These words define the mystery that was formulated before the foundation of the world. Eternal life depends exclusively on knowing the only true God and He who was sent, "who, being in the form of God, did not consider it robbery to be equal with God, but made Himself of no reputation, taking the form of a bondservant, and coming in the likeness of men. . . . He humbled Himself and became obedient to the point of death, even the death of the cross" (Philippians 2:6–8).

Transformation

Many Christians think that knowledge of God and our Lord Jesus Christ is nothing more than an intellectual exercise of traditional doctrines or biblical concepts. They have difficulty differentiating between the historical Jesus and Christ the Savior. Some venture to say that, by simply stating a prayer of confession and repentance, salvation is guaranteed. They speak as if salvation and eternal life are simply the results of memorizing "slogans" or the simple repetition of religious phrases.

What would be the meaning of this simple but indispensable phrase that defines salvation: "that they may know You"? Would it be to know the story of Jesus and what He did for humanity? Would it be to recognize God as the Supreme Being living in heaven and Jesus as the One sent in favor of men? Would it be to know biblical doctrines and have the ability to defend concepts that differ from other Christians? Or would it be to develop with God and with Christ, the Savior, an intimate relationship that is practical and real?

When you examine the prayer of Jesus found in John 17:3 and study the Greek word for "know" or "knowledge," you find concepts that may have come to us as a result of poor translations of the Bible. The Greek word carries a completely different meaning from the general understanding that salvation is acquired through knowledge of God, of doctrinal truths, and even the perception that because you attend a church, you are saved.

Let's analyze the topic again with this in mind: The Greek word for "know" used in this passage is *ginōskō*, and the meaning of this word changes the interpretation of the passage completely. *Ginōskō* means "to become acquainted with, to know." It is also the word used to describe the love and intimate relationship that exists between a husband and his wife where the man and his wife become one flesh (Genesis 2:24). Therefore, what Jesus actually expressed was this, "And this is eternal life, that they may know

Transformation Through Relationship

[*ginōskō*] . . . God, and Jesus Christ whom You have sent" (John 17:3). It is imperative for the Christian to develop a relationship of mutual love that is real and practical, which can be compared to the intimate relationship that exists in marriage. In this relationship, the two become one in a bond of unbreakable love with Christ. In other words, life eternal is that you "marry" Jesus, your spiritual husband. Only an intimate relationship with the Savior at this level will result in your salvation.

To develop this level of intimate relationship with God, you need to mature spiritually. Spiritual maturity comes as the result of practicing spiritual disciplines. This book will cover some of the spiritual disciplines, such as prayer, fasting, studying the Word of God, and stewardship. Let us also acknowledge that Jesus practiced all these spiritual disciplines during His life as He developed an intimate relationship with His Father and stayed in close communion with Heaven.

Transformation is spiritual maturity, and spiritual maturity is a change of paradigm in the life of the believer. For the apostle Paul, everything worth something became like "manure," which is the translation of the original Greek word when writing of the things he lost in order to possess the priceless treasure of knowing Christ. When we compare two similar statements that appear in Philippians 3:8–10, we find something extraordinary. In verse 8, the apostle states, "Yet indeed I also count all things loss for the excellence of the *knowledge* of Christ Jesus my Lord, for whom I have suffered the loss of all things, and count them as rubbish, that I may gain Christ" (emphasis added). Then, in verse 10, Paul repeats the sentiment when he says: "that I may *know* Him" (emphasis added). However, while it seems like Paul is saying the same thing using the same words, he isn't.

In his first statement, Paul is saying that he cannot compare anything with the incalculable value of the knowledge of Christ.

Transformation

The word that Paul uses in verse 8 is *gnōsis*, which means "knowledge, science, understanding," referring to general knowledge of the Christian religion. However, the word he uses in verse 10 has the same root as the word Jesus used in John 17:3, *ginōskō*. When Paul, using the limitations of human language, wants to express the kind of relationship he wants to develop with Jesus, he uses *ginōskō*. Paul wants to live with Jesus in an intimate communion where he can become one with Him. For Paul, Jesus was the greatest expression of knowledge and the most authentic experience of an intimate relationship, compared only to marriage, where two become one flesh. Human beings can never be satisfied by simply knowing about God. Truly knowing God can happen only through experience. We come to know God by experiencing Him in our lives and through the circumstances surrounding us.

The great men and women of God who knew the excellence of divine wisdom and developed an intimate relationship with God have traits in common. Those who live in an intimate relationship with Jesus perceive God as always working in the practical realities of their lives, find a real and personal love relationship with God, feel the call to serve God, and feel how God speaks to them through the Holy Spirit, through the Bible, prayer, circumstances, and the church. They clearly see God's ways and purposes for them; they will see them in trials and temptations, and this knowledge will carry them through the midst of crisis to make decisions that demand faith and action. They will have to make important adjustments in their lives so they can unite with God and find the right perspective of what it means to be a Christian. As they see God working in their lives and obey Him, they come to know God through these experiences.

The case of people not placing Jesus in the proper place in their lives is illustrated in one of the most important paintings by German painter Adolph Menzel (1815–1905), which hangs in

Transformation Through Relationship

the Berlin Art Gallery. This picture, although dedicated to King Frederick the Great, was not finished. In the painting, the famous artist intended to show Frederick talking to some of his generals. Menzel painted the generals and finished the background of the painting, leaving the figure of the king to be painted at the end. He traced Frederick's silhouette with charcoal but died before finishing the painting. For many Christians, Jesus is only a silhouette in the picture of their lives. They live without putting Jesus in the place He deserves. The church is part of the landscape, the background of the picture, but the presence of Christ is drawn only in charcoal. There is the intention to paint Him into their lives' pictures at some point. There is a desire to bring Him to the forefront of the life sooner or later. But life goes on with Jesus as a silhouette, a simple adornment or accessory.

The Bible teaches that an intimate relationship with God is the foundation of spiritual growth for Christians. There is a marked difference between knowing about God and developing an intimate love relationship with the Savior. Familiarity and intimacy are two different things. If one is confused with the other, you will have great problems. In marriage, familiarity occurs naturally and imperceptibly. On the other hand, intimacy is difficult to achieve. It should be deliberately sought and desired. Familiarity produces a state of comfort. Intimacy seeks a deeper understanding and results in an intense personal appreciation.

This difference is brought out in the story of what happened in a hospital room after a complicated facial operation on a young woman. The surgeon himself describes the scene:

> I stand by the bed where a young woman lies, her face postoperative, her mouth twisted in palsy, clownish. A tiny twig of the facial nerve, the one to the muscles of her mouth, has been severed. She will be thus from now

Transformation

on. The surgeon had followed with religious fervor the curve of her flesh; I promise you that. Nevertheless, to remove the tumor in her cheek, I had cut the little nerve.

Her young husband is in the room. He stands on the opposite side of the bed, and together they seem to dwell in the evening lamplight, isolated from me, private. Who are they, I ask myself, he and this wry-mouth I have made, who gaze at and touch each other so generously, greedily? The young woman speaks.

"Will my mouth always be like this?" she asks.

"Yes," I say, "it will. It is because the nerve was cut."

She nods, and is silent. But the young man smiles.

"I like it," he says, "It is kind of cute."

All at once I *know* who he is. I understand, and I lower my gaze. . . . Unmindful, he bends to kiss her crooked mouth, and I [am] so close I can see how he twists his own lips to accommodate to hers, to show her that their kiss still works.[1]

An intimate scene such as the one we have just read appears in Revelation 3:20. Jesus is at the door of your heart, and He is calling. He wants to live with you. "Behold, I stand at the door and knock. If anyone hears My voice and opens the door, I will come in to him and dine with him, and he with Me." This scene is a beautiful allegory that can help you understand the love of Jesus for you.

But how much does He love you? To understand this question, we need to study the original passage that inspires this metaphor. When John describes Jesus knocking at the door, he is referring to the poetry that appears in Song of Solomon 5. Read the passage carefully. Do not ignore a single word. First, the husband speaks:

Transformation Through Relationship

> I have come to my garden, my sister, my spouse;
> I have gathered my myrrh with my spice;
> I have eaten my honeycomb with my honey;
> I have drunk my wine with my milk (verse 1).

Then, the bride speaks:

> I sleep, but my heart is awake;
> It is the voice of my beloved! (verse 2).

She hears her husband knocking on the door:

> "Open for me, my sister, my love,
> My dove, my perfect one;
> For my head is covered with dew,
> My locks with the drops of the night" (verse 2).

The bride responds:

> I have taken off my robe;
> How can I put it on again?
> I have washed my feet;
> How can I defile them? (verse 3).

Then, the bride goes into detail:

> My beloved put his hand
> By the latch of the door,
> And my heart yearned for him.
> I arose to open for my beloved,
> And my hands dripped with myrrh,
> My fingers with liquid myrrh,
> On the handles of the lock.

Transformation

> I opened for my beloved,
> But my beloved had turned away and was gone.
> My heart leaped up when he spoke.
> I sought him, but I could not find him;
> I called him, but he gave me no answer.
> The watchmen who went about the city found me.
> They struck me, they wounded me;
> The keepers of the walls
> Took my veil away from me.
> I charge you, O daughters of Jerusalem,
> If you find my beloved,
> That you tell him I am lovesick! (verses 4–8).

To the Hebrews, these delicate and exquisite verses describe the love relationship of God with His people. For Christians, the husband's call to his wife reflects the indescribable love of Christ for His church. Throughout the Bible, this allegory appears again and again. God uses the terms *Father* and *Son* to describe the relationship that exists between the Divinity. But when it comes to describing in human terms the relationship He wants to have with us, He uses marriage, the most profound love relationship that leads us to merge with Him in a single mind and spirit. The Scripture uses the husband-wife figure to allude to the intimate relationship of love that God wants to develop with His people (this concept is found in Isaiah 62:5; Jeremiah 3:14; Hosea 2:16; Ephesians 5:25; and Revelation 19:7). This intimate relationship Jesus wants to develop with us is often compared to the union of marriage. We can count on unfailing love, sincere loyalty, and constant companionship in an intimate relationship with Jesus.

The illustration of Jesus knocking at the door means that He is calling His people, His church, and you. When the wife begins to make excuses, it is you who are making excuses. When the

Transformation Through Relationship

apathy of time extinguishes the passion of the first love, it is your apathy that separates you from the Beloved. Now we can better understand the allegory that appears in the call of the Faithful Witness to the church of Laodicea: "Behold, I stand at the door and knock. If anyone hears My voice and opens the door, I will come in to him and dine with him, and he with Me" (Revelation 3:20). We tend to use this verse to refer to the call of God to unbelievers; however, the correct context indicates that He is calling His church to open the door. The call is not for strangers; it is for the church. This call is for those who have settled in the warmth of an empty, superficial, and paltry relationship with Christ. Here is the message of Jesus for His wife, the church:

> "I know your works, that you are neither cold nor hot. I could wish you were cold or hot. So then, because you are lukewarm, and neither cold nor hot, I will vomit you out of My mouth. Because you say, 'I am rich, have become wealthy, and have need of nothing'—and do not know that you are wretched, miserable, poor, blind, and naked—I counsel you to buy from Me gold refined in the fire, that you may be rich; and white garments, that you may be clothed, that the shame of your nakedness may not be revealed; and anoint your eyes with eye salve, that you may see" (verses 15–18).

Jesus wants to develop an intimate relationship with you. Why do you leave Him standing out there, knocking on the door? The poet Lois Blanchard Eades makes a personal application of Revelation 3:20 when she writes:

> If Jesus came to your house to spend a day or two
> If He came unexpectedly, I wonder what you'd do.

Transformation

Oh, I know you'd give your nicest room to such an honored Guest,
And all the food you'd serve to Him would be the very best,
And you would keep assuring Him you're glad to have Him there—
That serving Him in your own home is joy beyond compare.

But when you saw Him coming, would you meet Him at the door
With arms outstretched in welcome to your heavenly Visitor?
Or would you have to change your clothes before you let Him in,
Or hide some magazines and put the Bible where they'd been?
Would you turn off the radio and hope He hadn't heard?
And wish you hadn't uttered that last, loud, hasty word?

Would you hide your worldly music and put some hymn books out?
Could you let Jesus walk right in, or would you rush about?
And I wonder—if the Savior spent a day or two with you,
Would you go right on doing the things you always do?
Would you keep right on saying the things you always say?
Would life for you continue as it does from day to day?

Would your family conversation keep up its usual pace?
And would you find it hard each meal to say a table grace?
Would you sing the songs you always sing, and read the books you read,
And let Him know the things on which your mind and spirit feed?

Transformation Through Relationship

Would you take Jesus with you everywhere you'd planned to go,
Or would you, maybe, change your plans for just a day or so?

Would you be glad to have Him meet your very closest friends,
Or would you hope they'd stay away until His visit ends?
Would you be glad to have Him stay forever on and on,
Or would you sigh with great relief when He at last was gone?
It might be interesting to know the things that you would do
If Jesus Christ in person came to spend some time with you.[2]

Reflection

Do you know Jesus enough that every detail of your existence is influenced by His life, by His death, by His words, by His promises, by His desire for your life? Is Jesus influencing every detail of your life, your family, your marriage, and your relationships at work and in the church? If not, what changes need to happen in your life?

---

1. Richard Selzer, *Mortal Lessons: Notes on the Art of Surgery* (New York: A Harvest Book, 1987), 45, 46.
2. Lois Blanchard Eades, "If Jesus Came to Your House," *If Jesus Came to Your House, and Other Poems* (Beacon, 1956).

Chapter 5

Transformation by Sanctification

The Bible teaches that an intimate relationship with God produces an inevitable transformation in the character of the Christian. The disciple of Christ must grow and mature into a deeper understanding of God and His will. The Scripture calls this process sanctification.

In the letter to the Hebrews, the author is writing to an audience that is supposed to have ample understanding of the Scriptures and exercise spiritual maturity as followers of Christ. However, that was not the case. The author has to explain the fundamentals of how to relate to Jesus and God's Word. In Hebrews 5:12 is the following declaration: "For though by this time you ought to be teachers, you need someone to teach you again the first principles of the oracles of God; and you have come to need milk and not solid food." Essentially, the author is saying, "It is necessary I teach you the basics about the gospel." He expected that those Christians would be mature in their understanding of the gospel, but they were still spiritual children.

Transformation

Christians should develop a character similar to that of Christ. Christians should learn to depend more and more on Jesus. Throughout this process, Christians also learn to distinguish the difference between what is important and what is trivial. Their faith is expected to develop, to build on the rock of the knowledge of God, to mature in the discernment between truth and error. Their faith must be strengthened. Their character must be polished. Their vocabulary, transformed. Their priorities should be clarified. Their trust in God, increased. However, many still act as breastfeeding infants, even after attending church for many years.

The Christian is called to mature, to grow, to connect theory with practice. But sadly, it is not difficult to find Christians who still drink milk after many years in the knowledge of the gospel. The author of Hebrews observes, "For though by this time you ought to be teachers, you need someone to teach you again the first principles of the oracles of God; and you have come to need milk and not solid food. For everyone who partakes only of milk is unskilled in the word of righteousness, for he is a babe. But solid food belongs to those who are of full age, that is, those who by reason of use have their senses exercised to discern both good and evil" (Hebrews 5:12–14). In short, Paul calls them spiritual infants (1 Corinthians 3:1, 2).

The Bible has many passages that describe this process of development and growth. However, far beyond describing the process, the Word tells us to put it into practice. For instance, in Matthew 5:48, Jesus commands us: "Be ye therefore perfect [*teleios*], even as your Father which is in heaven is perfect" (KJV). The word that the Bible translates as "perfect" or "finished" is *teleios*. This word is also translated in various places in the New King James Version as "mature." In 1 Corinthians 2:6: "We speak wisdom among those who are mature [*teleios*]." In 1 Corinthians 14:20, "Do not be children in understanding; however, in malice be babes, but in

Transformation by Sanctification

understanding be mature [*teleios*]." In Hebrews 5:14, "But solid food belongs to those who are of full age [*teleios*]." Also, the same word appears in the story of the rich young man in Matthew 19:21, "If you want to be perfect [*teleios*], go, sell what you have."

This profound and very important subject of being perfect is illuminated by Ellen G. White's comments. Sadly, too many Christians live miserable lives trying to become perfect and end up frustrated and depressed when they realize they are struggling with a sinful nature. How, then, can we reconcile these terms? Let us consider the following passages:

> He [Jesus] is a perfect and holy example, given for us to imitate. We cannot equal the pattern; but we shall not be approved of God if we do not copy it and, according to the ability which God has given, resemble it.[1]

> We cannot equal the example, but we should copy it.[2]

> We are to grow daily in spiritual loveliness. We shall fail often in our efforts to copy the divine pattern. We shall often have to bow down to weep at the feet of Jesus, because of our shortcomings and mistakes; but we are not to be discouraged.[3]

> He tells us to be perfect as He is, in the same manner. We are to be centers of light and blessing to our little circle, even as He is to the universe.[4]

> With our limited powers we are to be as holy in our sphere as God is holy in His sphere. To the extent of our ability, we are to make manifest the truth and love and excellence of the divine character.[5]

Transformation

> The faith of men in Christ as the Messiah was not to rest in the evidences of sight, and they believe on him because of his personal attractions, but because of the excellence of character found in him, which never had been, neither could be found in another.[6]

> There are many, especially among those who profess holiness, who compare themselves to Christ, as though they were equal with him in perfection of character. This is blasphemy. Could they obtain a view of Christ's righteousness, they would have a sense of their own sinfulness and imperfection.[7]

The Bible teaches that true perfection is only found in Christ. Jesus is our substitute and example. Our perfection depends solely and exclusively on Him.

> For in Him dwells all the fullness of the Godhead bodily; and you are complete in Him, who is the head of all principality and power (Colossians 2:9, 10).

> That we may present every man perfect in Christ Jesus (Colossians 1:28).

> For it pleased the Father that in Him all the fullness should dwell, and by Him to reconcile all things to Himself, by Him, whether things on earth or things in heaven, having made peace through the blood of His cross.
> And you, who once were alienated and enemies in your mind by wicked works, yet now He has reconciled in the body of His flesh through death, to present

Transformation by Sanctification

you holy, and blameless, and above reproach in His sight—if indeed you continue in the faith, grounded and steadfast, and are not moved away from the hope of the gospel which you heard, which was preached to every creature under heaven, of which I, Paul, became a minister (Colossians 1:19–23).

It seems the Bible is calling believers to spiritual growth, which is best understood as deepening maturity rather than a goal you have to reach. When the Bible refers to perfection (*teleios*), it speaks of the natural process of the discipleship of Christ. It is speaking of a sanctification growth that lasts a lifetime. A mature Christian develops characteristics that make a difference in daily living. This growth produces maturity, and maturity leaves its marks.

The first characteristic that is always noticeable in all mature Christians is discernment, which is the ability to distinguish between what is good and what is evil, to perceive a difference between truth and error.

The second characteristic noticed in a mature Christian is perseverance. When children learn to walk, they have no balance. They fall with ease. This is part of growing up. Human beings grow through challenges, work, and struggles. Mature Christians grow as they learn to trust in God. They understand why prayers are not answered magically or instantly. They understand that persistence in prayer, study, and meditation is designed for the benefit and growth of the believer. As Rabbi Abraham Heschel is said to have observed, "Faith like Job's cannot be shaken because it is the result of having been shaken."

The third characteristic noticed in a mature Christian is humility that includes the desire to continue to grow and mature. The more we grow and mature, the more we realize how far we are

Transformation

from the true perfection of Christ. Truly, "the closer you come to Jesus, the more faulty you will appear in your own eyes; for your vision will be clearer, and your imperfections will be seen in broad and distinct contrast to His perfect nature."[8]

Finally, sanctification is a process that lasts a lifetime. I'm reminded of an example told of a reporter who once asked renowned cellist Pablo Casals, "Mr. Casals, you are ninety-five years old and the greatest cellist that ever lived. Why do you still practice six hours a day?" Casals replied: "Because I think I am making progress."[9] In the same way, Christians should practice and exercise their faith daily.

Reflection

Does our salvation depend on our perfection?

---

1. Ellen G. White, *Testimonies for the Church*, vol. 2 (Mountain View, CA: Pacific Press®, 1948), 549.
2. White, 628.
3. Ellen G. White, *Selected Messages*, bk. 1 (Washington, DC: Review and Herald®, 1958), 337.
4. Ellen G. White, *Thoughts From the Mount of Blessing* (Mountain View, CA: Pacific Press®, 1956), 77.
5. White, *Selected Messages*, bk. 1, 337.
6. Ellen G. White, *The Spirit of Prophecy*, vol. 2 (Battle Creek, MI: Seventh-day Adventist Publishing Association, 1877), 39.
7. Ellen G. White, "In What Shall We Glory?" *Advent Review and Sabbath Herald*, March 15, 1887, 161, 162.
8. Ellen G. White, *Steps to Christ* (Washington, DC: Review and Herald®, 1977), 64.
9. This story about Pablo Casals is shared in many places. While his age at the time of the question differs, his response remains consistent.

Chapter 6

Transformation by Worship as a Lifestyle

Worship is at the very core of the reason for which we were created. God designed us to be worshipers. He does not want us just to set aside moments of worship as part of our lives; He wants our whole life to become a continuous experience of worship. Worship is not about a church service or singing hymns. It is not led by singers nor instruments. It isn't supposed to be a single part of the week or simply a time on Sabbath when we pause our lives to give God some time. Worship is the central focus of our lives at every moment, in every word, in every action. It should transform a meaningless life into purposeful living, from simple acts of worship to a commitment of the whole person. It's the orientation of our lives, which turns our face from worldly concerns toward God.

Worship is a life totally consumed by a passionate love for God. It is a life that focuses only on living close to and in accordance with the divine will. Of course, if we were created to worship, we can recognize that the attacks of Satan will be aimed at turning us into false worshipers. We first must understand what kind of

Transformation

worshipers there are. Paul categorizes humanity into three groups of worshipers—natural, spiritual, and carnal—when he explains, "But the natural man does not receive the things of the Spirit of God, for they are foolishness to him; nor can he know them, because they are spiritually discerned. But he who is spiritual judges all things, yet he himself is rightly judged by no one. . . . And I, brethren, could not speak to you as to spiritual people but as to carnal, as to babes in Christ" (1 Corinthians 2:14–3:1).

When we study this passage, we find that the apostle is suggesting that the natural people cannot discern the things of God because of their carnal nature. They have rejected God's eternal salvation through Christ and made their lives numb to the influence of the Holy Spirit. Blinded by selfishness and ignorant of what Jesus has done for them, they go through life dead in their sins with no desire for transformation.

The carnal person has accepted salvation by faith in Jesus but remains an infant in Christ. They are still governed by their flesh, bodies, and souls (mind, willpower, or emotions), but the Holy Spirit is working in them. Carnal Christians do not experience genuine worship because they're trapped in the things of this world. Their lives are made up of different fragments or portions: work, marriage, family, fun, hobbies, and rest, and to those they add time for church and congregational worship. Their relationship with God is just one more part of their existence.

For carnal people, worship is something they do, not something they are. It is a small slice of their lives. While worship has a place in their lives, it is not their life. That is why carnal people worship during church but never at home with their families or at work while earning a living. They consider it a necessary duty, usually for one or two hours on specific days of worship. Ask the carnal person, "Did you worship this week?" and the answer will surely be, "Of course, I went to church this week on Saturday morning."

Transformation by Worship as a Lifestyle

On the other hand, when the spiritual person is asked, "Have you worshiped this week?" the answer is going to be very different from that of the carnal person. The spiritual person will say: "My week has been full of worship. I have made mistakes, but I have worshiped God with all my heart."

Spiritual people are completely submitted to the Holy Spirit. They are guided by the Holy Spirit of God and worship continually because they have surrendered their whole lives. They live as true children of the Father in everything they do and say, "And because you are sons, God has sent forth the Spirit of His Son into your hearts, crying out, 'Abba, Father!' " (Galatians 4:6). Their desire to worship God is as intense on Monday morning as any other day. They worship God with as much passion at work and at home as in a church service. Instead of a part of their lives being about worship, spiritual people find that their whole lives are worship.

God wants us to commit ourselves completely. He does not want only a part of us. He asks for our hearts, souls, and minds and requires us to love Him with all our strength. God is not interested in half-hearted commitments, partial obedience, or the leftovers of our time and money. He wants our full devotion, not bits of our lives.

Worship appears continually in one form or another from Genesis to Revelation. It has been said that the theme of worship is closely related to fundamental issues of theology, such as creation, sin, the covenant, redemption, the people of God, and future hope. At the beginning of this world, the Word (John 1:1) formed creatures with His hands, in His image and likeness (Genesis 2:7; 1:26), for the purpose that they should worship Him for eternity. All worship of God must come from a heart full of love for Him and for those who gather to worship. The Word is clear: "He who does not love does not know God, for God is love" (1 John 4:8).

Transformation

When the church meets to worship, it does so on the basis of brotherly love. True worship is born from a heart full of love. It would be wrong to come into the presence of the Lord while holding a grudge in your heart. The first step toward true worship as a church is reaching relationships that honor the new commandment "love one another" (John 15:12). We are called to practice recognizing the presence of Jesus in our midst and knowing when we are living together in reciprocal love. We must also know when we have lost Him by letting ourselves be led astray by differences. True worship requires the presence of Jesus, and He is present only in an environment of real communion based on love among believers. "No one has seen God at any time. If we love one another, God abides in us, and His love has been perfected in us" (1 John 4:12).

In relation to worship in church services, questions arise: Does God prefer any particular style of worship? Is there a way of worship that is better than another? Is there a universally appropriate form to be followed? The Bible makes it clear that neither the form nor the style of worship in itself is important to God. What God seeks is the condition and attitude of the worshiper. The highest expectation is, in the eyes of God, "a broken spirit, a broken and a contrite heart" (Psalm 51:17). But contrition must be accompanied by a life that seeks "to do justly, to love mercy, and to walk humbly with your God" (Micah 6:8). Therefore, only genuine transformation of the heart will guarantee genuine worship. Whatever the format, if people do not come to church with a transformed heart, worship will have no meaning. Worship is much more than the act of coming to church. It becomes a way of life.*

---

* In the Bible, we find a plethora of expressions of worship: Psalms 26:7; 28:7; 47:1; 71:23, 24; 95:6; 98:4; 100:1; 132:9; Exodus 15:20, 21; Ephesians 5:19; Colossians 3:16; Psalms 33:8; 135:1; 134:2; 143:6; Philippians 2:10; 2 Samuel 6:14; Jeremiah 31:13; Psalm 126:2, 3; Acts 3:8; Revelation 19:7; Psalm 150; Ecclesiastes 3:4; Psalm 46:10; Nehemiah 8:10; Job 8:20, 21; Joshua 6:2–5; 2 Chronicles 20:20–22.

Transformation by Worship as a Lifestyle

True worship becomes real throughout the week, when you offer someone a glass of cold water, when you love someone who is hard to love, when you practice faithfulness, and with many other integral actions and attitudes. True worshipers value worship to God as an essential charge, define their priorities in accordance with divine priorities, and are certain that everything they do is for the glory of God. They do not cling to personal desires, carnal ambitions, or the human need for recognition. They know nothing can compare to being with the Lord, preferring one day in His courts over a thousand days away from them (Psalm 84:10). They choose the best part, which will never be taken from them (Luke 10:42) and can rise from the Lord's feet after they have washed them with tears of love (Luke 7:38) and deal with the normal chores of every human being, yet now with a heavenly perspective.

To worship is to live in communion with God as a way of life. However, it is also the specific moment of deep intimacy with our Lord in which the alabaster bottle of perfume from our heart is broken at His feet. There's a need to spend these daily moments with the Lord, just as the husband and wife need to be together to love and express love in a variety of ways. Something special occurs in your life when you experience the presence of God, which could well be called "living in a state of worship." This living in a state of worship is the consequence of being a true worshiper and in no way replaces the specific act of worshiping God in spirit and truth. It means separating an exclusive time to be with Him and love Him. To live in a state of worship is to live in such a way that all thoughts, attitudes, and actions of every moment are accepted by God as worship in His name. Living in a state of worship refers to living worshipfully beyond the hours of worship as if we never left. It is to live in private what you live in public. It is to act in a way that you can present your actions

Transformation

to God without having anything to be ashamed of because, with each of them, you strive to glorify the Lord.

Living a life of worship means that with your work, you worship Him; with your free time, you worship Him; with your conversations, you worship Him; in silence, you worship Him; and with your motivations, you worship Him. This lifestyle is not living "religiously" but striving to live in such a way that nothing that is thought, said, done, or left undone offends God in any way. As the Bible says, "Whatever you do, do all to the glory of God" (1 Corinthians 10:31). True worship is more than listening to a sermon, lifting hands, standing still during praises, returning tithes and giving offerings, or spending three hours a week in church. Rather than rituals or things we occasionally do, worship is a way of life.

In one way or another, we all worship. Even unbelievers worship something, whether it be money, music or sports idols, or fame. We were created to worship. Look at the Creation story: the fact that God created Adam and Eve on the sixth day, just before the Sabbath, has profound theological and sociological significance. The Creator intended that worship should have priority over every other activity. This priority demands that the followers of God not only worship but also worship correctly. The act and manner of worship cannot be taken for granted.

Worship that pleases God has these three characteristics: First, it is grounded in the truth. We cannot simply create our own image of God that is comfortable to our personal understanding. That is idolatry. Worship must be based on the truth of Scripture. It is not about our opinion of God but about what the Word has revealed about Him. "True worshipers will worship the Father in spirit and truth; for the Father is seeking such to worship Him" (John 4:23). To "worship in truth" is to worship God as the Bible truly reveals Him.

Transformation by Worship as a Lifestyle

Second, God is pleased with authentic and practical worship. When we worship, God looks beyond our words, observing the attitude of the heart. "Man looks at the outward appearance, but the Lord looks at the heart" (1 Samuel 16:7). True worship occurs when our spirit responds to God Himself, not to a melody. The emotions produced by music in a worship service are often confused with those given by the Holy Spirit, but they are not the same. In fact, some sentimental and introspective songs hinder worship instead of bringing us closer to God; what the music really achieves is stimulating our feelings. When Jesus said that we should "worship in spirit" (John 4:24), He referred to our spirit, not the Holy Spirit. We were created in the image of God and, therefore, are spiritual creatures. He designed us so that we could communicate with Him. Worship is the response of our spirit to the Spirit of God. When we worship, the most distracting factor is ourselves: our interests and concerns about the impression we give.

Third, God loves rational worship. Jesus' command to "love God with all your mind" is repeated three times in the New Testament (Matthew 22:37; Mark 12:30; Luke 10:27). God is not pleased with our enthusiastic "Amen," singing solely hymns, apathetic prayers, or exclamations of indifference and void of any thinking. If we do not think about what we do when we are worshiping, worship makes no sense. By offering our "rational worship" to God, it is our privilege to "worship with understanding." Our mind must be focused on what we are doing. God would prefer that we speak only one word with understanding than speak many incoherent phrases that make no sense (1 Corinthians 14).

Remember, Christians, like ancient Israel, are called to

> "Hear, O Israel: The Lord our God, the Lord is one!
> You shall love the Lord your God with all your heart,
> with all your soul, and with all your strength.

Transformation

"And these words which I command you today shall be in your heart. You shall teach them diligently to your children, and shall talk of them when you sit in your house, when you walk by the way, when you lie down, and when you rise up. You shall bind them as a sign on your hand, and they shall be as frontlets between your eyes. You shall write them on the doorposts of your house and on your gates" (Deuteronomy 6:4–9).

Reflection
How will you cultivate a lifestyle of worship in your life?

Chapter 7

Transformation Is Conversion

What is conversion? There is no specific definition of the word *conversion* in Scripture. In Hebrew, the word used is *shwb* and in Greek, *epistrephō*. In both cases, the meaning is the same: "to turn, return, be converted, turn back." In short, conversion is a change of direction, but this is not entirely clear in the Bible. The Bible defines what faith is in clear terms. *Love* is also masterfully defined by Paul, John, and James. But while *grace, justification, sanctification, the plan of salvation,* and *forgiveness* are well presented concepts throughout the Bible, this is not the case with *conversion*. No text defines it clearly. What we can find is the Bible's description of what happens when a person is converted. Conversion is not just a change of direction; it is also looking in another direction. "Repent, then, and turn to (*epistrephō*) God, so that your sins may be wiped out, that times of refreshing may come from the Lord, and that he may send the Messiah, who has been appointed for you—even Jesus" (Acts 3:19, 20, NIV).

I once encountered a story about a bartender who liked good

Transformation

music and decided to attend one of John Wesley's lectures to hear the songs. He had decided to listen to the music but not the sermon. So he sat with his head between his legs, fingers in his ears as Wesley began to preach. However, when God wants to speak to someone's heart, He finds a way. A fly flew over this man's head and landed on his nose. When he tried to scare away the fly, he heard nine words that changed his life. He heard Wesley say, "He that hath ears to hear, let him hear." From that moment, he had no rest in his soul. He returned the next night, listened attentively, and was converted.

In the experience of conversion, at least five things begin to happen in your life that are significant for a practical relationship with Jesus.

First, at conversion, you receive a new nature, which is the most transformative and revolutionary aspect of conversion. The new nature causes a change of direction and life that is so fundamental that, in speaking with Nicodemus (John 3), Jesus expressed it as being born again. Conversion is a new birth of water and the Spirit. A converted person does not say, "I do what I want," but instead, "I will do what God teaches me." The most impressive thing is they do not say this by imposition or obligation but on the basis of a new relationship of love that has been born within. To fulfill the will of God is now a delight, and to imitate Jesus is the deepest desire of his or her heart.

Second, at conversion, you obtain a deep desire to know the teachings of the Word of God and their implications in Christian life. You enter the kingdom of God like a child. You may have received religious training, but you still may not know how to apply these teachings of Jesus to your practical life. Although you enter into a new kind of life through conversion and have experienced a deep and genuine encounter, you will be eager to know and study the Scriptures to find what God expects of

Transformation Is Conversion

you. The experience of conversion is neither superficial nor a mechanical relationship. Conversion is not a frivolous acceptance of a religious formula. "Therefore, if anyone is in Christ, the new creation has come: The old has gone, the new is here!" (2 Corinthians 5:17, NIV). This does not in any way eliminate our emotions and feelings, but when the individual takes on a new nature, something has to change in his life. It goes from egocentrism to putting God at the center of his or her life. New desires, hopes, and ideals are born within the heart.

Third, at conversion, you obtain a deep desire to follow the teachings of the Word of God and to live a new experience, no matter the price you have to pay. The desire to know, however good it may be, is not enough. There must be an undeniable longing to *follow* the Word. This is not as simple as it seems. Living the Christian life would be relatively easy if it only meant accepting religious standards and attending church. Unfortunately, this idea is more prevalent among us than we want to admit. But if conversion means applying Christian ideals in a way that leads the individual to go beyond what is accepted by society or religious standards, then living the Christian life becomes one of the most sublime and beautiful tasks in which a human being can participate.

Fourth, at conversion, you receive power that goes beyond human power. God gives us His power through the presence of His Holy Spirit and enables us to follow the teachings of Jesus Christ. Many of Jesus' teachings go against our logic, our human desires, and our passions. It is not natural for us to love our enemies, to do good to those who hate and persecute us, or to forgive those who falsely speak of us. Therefore, to understand Jesus and live like Him, we need power from above. Jesus promised us the presence of the Holy Spirit. That power will sustain us in the hour of trial.

Fifth, at conversion, we receive the proper foundation and

Transformation

motivation to live a practical life, not in the flesh but in the Spirit. It is possible that many are following the teachings of Jesus without the right motives. Some teachers and preachers are satisfied with answers that scarcely bear the seal of Christ because it is easier to lead people to practice external forms of religion than to lead them to a permanent encounter with Jesus that causes them to say to God, "Not my will, but yours." The standards of a Christian life are high and often conflict with our human passions. Therefore, a decision is required. The life of every Christian must be firmly grounded in a genuine relationship with Christ.

Being converted does not mean that we are perfect, but we are different. Jesus accepts us and helps us change our direction. From the point where you are, you are going to turn and start walking in the opposite direction. Some Christians fear that God does not accept them, that their relationship with Jesus is broken every time they sin. It is true that the sinner who rebels against God cannot expect to have a relationship with Jesus. But there is a marked difference between the person who rebels against God and the person who has repented of his sins and is trying to overcome them. "When it is in the heart to obey God, when efforts are put forth to this end, Jesus accepts this disposition and effort as man's best service, and he makes up for the deficiency with his own divine merit."[1]

The greatest and most sublime task of the Holy Spirit is to guide, to convince, to touch the hardest fibers of human consciousness. The Holy Spirit leads the individual into an experience through which he can come to know Jesus, the Savior. This experience will gradually lead him to grow in His image and likeness. This is conversion as we defined above: a change of direction.

Transformation is also about learning from our failures. A

Transformation Is Conversion

story has been told about Thomas Edison, who performed three thousand experiments in his effort to make an electric light bulb. When he had done fifteen hundred failed experiments, a reporter is said to have asked him, "Do you not think you should give up your effort to make a light bulb?" To which he replied, "I have not failed 1,500 times, I have successfully discovered 1,500 ways *not* to make a light bulb." What does "experimenting" mean in our relationship with Jesus? Among other things, it means we will learn from our own mistakes. It is difficult to understand that Edison's three-thousandth experiment succeeded. But it would have been impossible for him to jump from the first experiment to the three-thousandth. The 2,999 previous experiments were a success as well because, from each of them, Edison learned what not to do to create a light bulb. In the same way, Christians can learn from their failures to achieve success.

Commenting on conversion, Saint Augustine made the following observation,

> Late have I loved you, beauty so old and so new: late have I loved you. And see, you were within and I was in the external world and sought you there, and in my unlovely state I plunged into those lovely created things which you made. You were with me, and I was not with you. The lovely things kept me far from you, though if they did not have their existence in you, they had no existence at all. You called and cried out loud and shattered my deafness. You were radiant and resplendent, you put to flight my blindness. You were fragrant, and I drew in my breath and now pant after you. I tasted you, and I feel but hunger and thirst for you. You touched me, and I am set on fire to attain the peace which is yours.[2]

Transformation

When we want to obey and are trying to obey, this is experimental religion. Far from rejecting us because we make mistakes, Jesus accepts our efforts and the best we have to offer and immediately applies His merits to our failures. Our relationship with Him remains intact; it does not break. The idea that the Christian breaks his relationship with Jesus every time he sins is actually a subtle way of saying we are saved by works. It makes obedience, rather than faith, the condition of our acceptance by God.

Conversion involves a change of direction. There is no conversion without a change of life and commitment to the Lord. This means that we will continually test the ways of living a Christian life until we discover that it works, with the assurance that Jesus walks by our side at all times, helping us to learn even from our weaknesses.

Reflection

Consider your conversion. How do you continue to experience—or, like Edison, experiment with—conversion today?

---

1. Ellen G. White, "Faith and Works," *Signs of the Times*, June 16, 1890.
2. Saint Augustine, *Confessions*, trans. Henry Chadwick (New York: Oxford University Press, 1991), 201.

Chapter 8

Transformation Through Bible Study

Spiritual disciplines cannot become mandatory tasks performed in order to win the favor of God. Viewing the disciplines this way will result in a legalistic religion, and you will lose the ability to develop a living relationship with God. Jesus practiced all spiritual disciplines, not to receive more favor from God but because He already counted on His favor and these were meant to keep Him connected to Heaven. Christians practice spiritual disciplines as a result of having been reached by the love and grace of God, not to achieve a goal.

To develop an intimate relationship with God, you need to study the Bible systematically. The purpose of studying the Scriptures is not to gather more information but to know God intimately. In His Word, you can discover His love and the plan of salvation for humanity. As you study it, you discover His will and allow God to transform your life through His revelation. When you study the Bible and pray, God shows you what to do, what to change, and the spiritual context in which you find yourself in

Transformation

relation to the Savior, your family, and your church.

The Bible deals with many topics. It is about God, human beings, and the relationship between God and humanity. But the most outstanding thing is the divine plan to restore the broken relationship between God and humanity. This means that the Bible contains theology, history, and ethics because the main narrative is about God's various attempts to redeem or save His people. The central story in the Bible is rightly called the story of salvation.

The Scripture clearly reveals that it is necessary for us to stay connected with God through His Word. Through daily study of the Bible, we can hear the voice of our God. The Word of God is food for the soul, as Jesus Himself said to Satan when He was tempted in the wilderness: "It is written: 'Man shall not live by bread alone, but by every word that proceeds from the mouth of God' " (Matthew 4:4). Many think that in order to live, we only need physical food. We do, but spiritual hunger can be satisfied only with the Word of God.

The Bible is not a book that was relevant only for the time in which it was written; it is a book for today and forever. Commenting on this, the great evangelist Dwight L. Moody said:

> A great many people seem to think that the Bible is out of date, that it is an old book, and they think it has passed its day. They say it was very good for the dark ages, and that there is some very good history in it, but it was not intended for the present time; we are living in a very enlightened age and men can get on very well without the old book; we have outgrown it. Now you might just as well say that the sun, which has shone so long, is now so old that it is out of date, and that whenever a man builds a house he need not put any windows in it, because we have a newer light

and a better light; we have gaslight and electric light. These are something new; and I would advise people, if they think the Bible is too old and worn out, when they build houses, not to put windows in them, but just to light them with electric light; that is something new and that is what they are anxious for.[1]

Most books go out of style, but the Bible is and always will be the book of books. The Bible is the revelation of God. There is nothing more satisfying and exciting than knowing God. It is a privilege you should not miss. Only God can fill your life. A famous thought attributed to Saint Jerome states: "When we pray, we speak to God, but when we read Scripture, God speaks to us." We must study the Bible because it is the source of truth, happiness, and victory. Bible study is your primary defense against temptation, discouragement, depression, and feelings of guilt, anger, and rage. It is your spiritual food in which you must take part daily. When you open your heart to the voice of God through the Word, you grow spiritually, you understand God's plan for your life, and you feel joy even when facing difficult times in your life.

The Lord wants you to set aside a specific time every day to be dedicated to the study of His Word. There are many reasons to read and study God's message through His Word. Ellen G. White enumerates many of them:

Confirm the truth. "There is no excuse for anyone in taking the position that there is no more truth to be revealed, and that all our expositions of Scripture are without an error. The fact that certain doctrines have been held as truth for many years by our people, is not a proof that our ideas are infallible. Age will not make error into truth, and truth can afford to be fair. No true doctrine will lose anything by close investigation."[2]

Transformation

Develop the understanding. "There will be a development of the understanding, for the truth is capable of constant expansion. . . .

". . . Our exploration of the truth is yet incomplete. We have gathered up only a few rays of light."[3]

The only source for doctrines and reform. "But God will have a people upon the earth to maintain the Bible, and the Bible only, as the standard of all doctrines and the basis of all reforms."[4]

Endure trials and confusion. "In order to endure the trial before them, they must understand the will of God as revealed in His word. . . . None but those who have fortified the mind with the truths of the Bible will stand through the last great conflict. To every soul will come the searching test: Shall I obey God rather than men? The decisive hour is even now at hand. Are our feet planted on the rock of God's immutable Word? Are we prepared to stand firm in defense of the commandment of God and the faith of Jesus?"[5]

Avoid clinging to traditions by denying investigation of the Scripture. "As real spiritual life declines, it has ever been the tendency to cease to advance in the knowledge of the truth. Men rest satisfied with the light already received from God's word, and discourage any further investigation of the Scriptures."[6]

Continue spiritual growth. "When God's people are at ease, and satisfied with their present enlightenment, we may be sure that He will not favor them. It is His will that they should be ever moving forward, to receive the increased and ever-increasing light which is shining for them."[7]

Clearly, the Word of God came by divine inspiration. Jesus Himself came to fulfill the Scripture, not to change it or abolish it.

Transformation happens through the study of God's Word because God Himself reveals His Word for you so you may know Him. Jesus appeals to believers to scrutinize the Holy Scriptures. God wants you to fulfill His Word, put it into practice, and share

Transformation Through Bible Study

it with others. God desires that you study His Word deeply so you can fight against falsehood and ignorance. When you study the Bible, you find the security of salvation in Christ. Studying the Holy Scriptures gives you joy and peace and enables you to express your faith. Studying the Bible gives you confidence and power in prayer. It makes you realize the forgiveness of your sins through the sacrifice of Christ. If you feel lost, studying the Bible will bring you back to God. Bible study instructs and prepares you for every good work.

Reflection
Consider making the following commitment regarding the study of God's Word: From now on, I am determined, before the Lord, to _____ .

---

1. D. L. Moody, *Pleasure and Profit in Bible Study* (New York: Fleming H. Revell, 1895), 10, 11.
2. Ellen G. White, *Counsels to Writers and Editors* (Nashville, TN: Southern Publishing Association, 1946), 35.
3. Ellen G. White, Letter 156, 1903.
4. Ellen G. White, *The Great Controversy* (Nampa, ID: Pacific Press®, 2005), 595.
5. White, 593, 594.
6. White, *Counsels to Writers and Editors*, 39.
7. White, 41.

Chapter 9

Transformation Through Prayer

To develop an intimate relationship with God, you must recognize that prayer is an essential tool in your spiritual life. Prayer is a mental attitude of openness to God to communicate with Him and He with you, even if you do not have a formal conversation. That direct channel will never have interference. This is what is meant by "pray without ceasing" (1 Thessalonians 5:17).

Prayer is a discipline. All disciplines require effort and dedication because they do not come naturally. As you practice, it becomes a habit and a part of life. Consider this statement:

> No other life was ever so crowded with labor and responsibility as was that of Jesus; yet how often He was found in prayer! How constant was His communion with God! Again and again in the history of His earthly life are found records such as these: "Rising up a great while before day, He went out, and departed into a solitary place, and there prayed." . . .

Transformation

> . . . As one with us, a sharer in our needs and weaknesses, He was wholly dependent upon God, and in the secret place of prayer He sought divine strength, that He might go forth braced for duty and trial. In a world of sin Jesus endured struggles and torture of soul. In communion with God He could unburden the sorrows that were crushing Him. Here He found comfort and joy.
>
> . . . As a man He supplicated the throne of God till His humanity was charged with a heavenly current that should connect humanity with divinity.[1]

There are times in our lives when all we have left to do is pray. We find ourselves cornered by circumstances and devoid of human responses. It is in moments like these that we turn our eyes to Heaven and humbly ask for God's intervention in our lives. However, if we are sincere with ourselves, we must acknowledge that we often seek God at the last moment. We seek Him when our human strength and methods have reached their limits and we realize that we cannot move forward. We look for Him when we lose sleep and our life is entangled more and more in the intricate webs of the situations of a world in constant change.

How much we need prayer! It is an indispensable instrument for the Christian. Christ Himself was in constant communion with the Father through prayer. How many of us need this heavenly current? How many of us need the life that comes from God through continuous communion?

Great men and women of God were always men and women of prayer. One great man of prayer is George Mueller. One day, Mueller looked out onto Bristol Street from the window of his home in England and saw abandoned children living on the streets. He was so moved that he decided to start an orphanage

Transformation Through Prayer

to help them. Over the course of his life, George Mueller cared for more than ten thousand orphans. In his journals, Mueller told fascinating stories of answered prayers. He kept a record of all his prayers, and what's most remarkable is that his notes show more than fifty thousand answered prayers.[2] Time after time, God answered the prayers of George Mueller. God wants to answer our prayers as well.

Stories in the Word confirm that God is attentive to our prayers and responds in a wonderful way. One of these stories is in the book of Daniel. Many of us read Daniel with an emphasis on prophecies, beasts, and times. However, the book of the prophet Daniel collects stories we often overlook. Daniel's prayer in chapter 9 is probably one of the most beautiful confession and intercessory prayers ever recorded. The story also accounts that while Daniel was still praying, God commanded the angel Gabriel to answer the prayer immediately and sent him with the following message: "At the beginning of your supplications the command went out, and I have come to tell you, for you are greatly beloved" (Daniel 9:23). How comforting it is to know that Heaven draws near to Earth. God is close to you. You are loved!

Daniel's story is full of references that make us understand why he was so loved by God. It also highlights his prayer life from the moment he decided to be different from the other young men of the kingdom to when he was thrown into the lions' den for keeping his daily prayer times. If Daniel had kept a prayer book like Mueller's, how many experiences would he have written!

Daniel's story in chapter 9 pulls back the curtain on angelic activity in response to prayer. If we could run the curtain, we would see how the angels of God fight with the powers of evil to answer our prayers. The evil angels contend for the souls, and the angels of God resist them. The power of a simple prayer is revealed in the following quotation: "Satan cannot endure to

Transformation

have his powerful rival appealed to, for he fears and trembles before [Christ's] strength and majesty. At the sound of fervent prayer, Satan's whole host trembles. He continues to call legions of his evil angels to accomplish his object. And when angels, all-powerful, clothed with the armory of heaven, come to the help of the fainting, pursued soul, Satan and his host fall back, well knowing that their battle is lost."[3] Similarly,

> The conflict was severe. Evil angels were crowding about them, corrupting the atmosphere with their poisonous influence, and stupefying their sensibilities. Holy angels were anxiously watching these souls and were waiting to drive back Satan's host. . . .
>
> If Satan sees he is in danger of losing one soul, he will exert himself to the utmost to keep that one. And when the individual is aroused to his danger, and, with distress and fervor, looks to Jesus for strength, Satan fears he shall lose a captive, and he calls a reinforcement of his angels to hedge in the poor soul, and form a wall of darkness around him, that heaven's light may not reach him. But if the one in danger perseveres, and in helplessness and weakness casts himself upon the merits of the blood of Christ, Jesus listens to the earnest prayer of faith, and sends a reinforcement of those angels which excel in strength to deliver him.[4]

I once encountered a story about the first Christians converted in Africa, who were known for being men of prayer. Each of them had a separate place in the jungle where they daily poured out their hearts to God. Over time, paths were worn into the ground, and the grass did not grow there. As a result, when one of them began to waver in their daily fellowship with God and

Transformation Through Prayer

began to be negligent in prayer, the other brothers realized that the grass was beginning to regrow. With affection, they reminded the negligent: "Brother, the grass grows in your path; you need to return to daily communion with God." I wonder: How many of us have allowed the path of our relationship with God to be filled with grass? How many of us have forgotten the trail that leads us to that necessary and continuous dialogue with God? How many of us have abandoned the path?

Reflection
Consider whether your pathway to prayer is clear. Have you allowed grass to grow over the pathway? How can you make sure the pathway remains clear?

---

1. Ellen G. White, *The Desire of Ages* (Nampa, ID: Pacific Press®, 2005), 362, 363.

2. Donald S. Whitney, "What George Mueller Can Teach Us About Prayer," *Crossway*, July 27, 2015, https://www.crossway.org/articles/what-george-mueller-can-teach-us-about-prayer/.

3. Ellen G. White, "The Power of Satan," *Advent Review, and Sabbath Herald*, May 13, 1862, 187.

4. Ellen G. White, *Messages to Young People* (Washington, DC: Review and Herald®, 1980), 52, 53.

Chapter 10

Transformation Through Fasting

One of the spiritual disciplines that will help you develop an intimate relationship with God is fasting. True biblical fasting, despite being misused by legalists, was never intended to become a practice for gaining merit. It is not intended to win God's favor or become an act of penance. True fasting does not bring God closer to man; it brings man closer to God. The Word of God teaches us about fasting:

> "Why have we fasted," they say,
>   "and you have not seen it?
> Why have we humbled ourselves,
>   and you have not noticed?"

> "Yet on the day of your fasting, you do as you please
>   and exploit all your workers.
> Your fasting ends in quarreling and strife,
>   and in striking each other with wicked fists.

Transformation

> You cannot fast as you do today
>   and expect your voice to be heard on high.
> Is this the kind of fast I have chosen,
>   only a day for people to humble themselves?
> Is it only for bowing one's head like a reed
>   and for lying in sackcloth and ashes?
> Is that what you call a fast,
>   a day acceptable to the Lord?"
>
> "Is not this the kind of fasting I have chosen:
> to loose the chains of injustice
>   and untie the cords of the yoke,
> to set the oppressed free
>   and break every yoke?
> Is it not to share your food with the hungry
>   and to provide the poor wanderer with shelter—
> when you see the naked, to clothe them,
>   and not to turn away from your own flesh and blood?"
>   (Isaiah 58:3–7, NIV).

In the Bible, fasting is not mandated. There is not a single statement in the Bible that one can interpret as binding. Fasting is not a way to spirituality; rather, it is a means to lead you to reflection and dependence on the Giver of all things. It is false to think that you are more spiritual simply because you fast every month, every week, or twice a week (like the Pharisees). Fasting holds no value as a religious ceremony. "All the fasting in the world will not take the place of simple trust in the word of God. 'Ask,' He says, 'and ye shall receive.' "[1] And, "The true fast is no mere formal service."[2]

Jesus fasted occasionally, but He wasn't governed by a religious calendar. He did not teach that fasting was a way to impress

Transformation Through Fasting

others; in fact, He told His followers not to advertise when they fasted. Fasting is not spiritual blackmail, a hunger strike, or a symbol of great spirituality. When you fast, you must humble yourself and let go of all rancor, pride, anger, lies, idolatry, and lack of love. In this way, fasting becomes a means of cleansing the heart and promoting a good disposition. You will get an answer to your prayers because you humbled your soul before God. Jesus said, "When you fast, do not look somber as the hypocrites do, for they disfigure their faces to show others they are fasting. Truly I tell you, they have received their reward in full. But when you fast, put oil on your head and wash your face, so that it will not be obvious to others that you are fasting, but only to your Father, who is unseen; and your Father, who sees what is done in secret, will reward you" (Matthew 6:16–18, NIV).

When fasting, consider the following that will help you enjoy this meaningful spiritual discipline:

Set a specific goal. Why do you fast? Is it to obtain spiritual renewal or to ask for direction, healing, a solution to problems, or special grace to face a difficult situation? Keeping your mind on the right perspective will help you continue your fast when physical desires or daily pressures tempt you to give up.

Prepare spiritually. The foundation of fasting and prayer is repentance. Unconfessed sin hinders your relationship with God. Throughout Scripture, we find that God's response always comes after genuine repentance. Ask the Holy Spirit to reveal to you whatever is in your heart that does not please God and claim the promise of 1 John 1:9, "If we confess our sins, he is faithful and just and will forgive us our sins and purify us from all unrighteousness" (NIV).

Prepare physically. Do not rush into a fast. If you plan to abstain from food, you will find it useful to start reducing your food intake before you abstain completely. This sends a signal to your

Transformation

mind that you have entered a time of fasting. Physical preparation for fasting facilitates the drastic alteration in your daily diet. If you plan to fast, you must do it according to the instructions of Jesus. Do not advertise that you are fasting. The fast practiced by Christians is not something done weekly or on a certain day but on occasion as warranted by your moral and spiritual situation. Fasting is always accompanied by fervent prayer to God.

Choose the type of fast. It's not just about not eating; there are many types of fasts. The purpose is to withdraw and dedicate a special time to the Lord. It's a special time for you to immerse yourself in prayer, Bible reading, praise, and worship. Otherwise, fasting is not a spiritual experience. Spiritual fasting is the act of voluntarily abstaining from anything that can distract you from desperately seeking God.

Focus your time. Set aside a large amount of time to be alone with the Lord during your fast. The longer you are with Him in communion, worship, and devotion, and the more you read and meditate on His Word during this time, the more intimacy you will develop with God.

Benefit from the fast. Fasting takes you out of the turmoil and bustle of everyday life so you can listen to the Holy Spirit. It brings you into a posture of humility by confronting attitudes of pride and spiritual arrogance. It gives you the strength to win spiritual battles that you would never win without the attitudes and perspective gained by fasting.

Fasting is not limited to abstaining from food for a period of time. In fact, fasting includes deciding to refrain from being continuously connected to the news, choosing to abstain from radio and television, or refraining from using your phone, email, and text messages for twenty-four hours. It also includes times when you follow the "Daniel diet," which is eating only whole foods, like fruits and vegetables.

Transformation Through Fasting

Reflection
What characteristics are used to describe true fasting? Does it have to do with giving up something or with the attitude of the spirit?

---

1. Ellen G. White, *Counsels on Diet and Foods* (Hagerstown, MD: Review and Herald®, 2001), 189.
2. Ellen G. White, *The Desire of Ages* (Nampa, ID: Pacific Press®, 2005), 278.

Chapter 11

Transformation Through Journaling

Another spiritual discipline that will help you develop an intimate relationship with God is journaling. Keeping a journal is a unique spiritual journey that documents your life and helps you take a closer look at yourself, your faith, and your walk with Jesus. Most humans tend to forget life experiences and lessons that help us grow. Writing down meaningful experiences allows you to recall your journey through life in a systematic way. If you are committed to growing spiritually, to being more like Jesus, and to living by grace, the discipline of keeping a journal can be very useful. It can help you take a spiritual inventory of what really makes the difference in your relationship with God, as the Bible counsels, "Finally, brothers and sisters, whatever is true, whatever is noble, whatever is right, whatever is pure, whatever is lovely, whatever is admirable—if anything is excellent or praiseworthy—think about such things" (Philippians 4:8, NIV).

As a spiritual discipline, keeping a journal is about recording your experiences with God. It can include prayers, requests,

Transformation

questions, and any answers given. You can write down your thoughts and what you are learning in your daily study of the Word.

However, a spiritual journal should not be confused with an exact outline of what happens to you each day, although you may include descriptions of some events. This type of spiritual exercise focuses more on the inner life, on the experiences you have in your intimate relationship with God. It serves not only as a record but also as an opportunity to reflect more deeply on how the Lord works in your life. Keeping a journal has many benefits:

> When I first began to journal, I felt self-conscious. I had visions of everyone stealing a peek at what I was writing . . . and laughing. I had fears that my journal would reveal what I was sure everyone already suspected: that I was a shallow person.
>
> But slowly my reluctances lost their hold on me, and I found myself recording in the journal, more and more, the thoughts that flooded my inner spirit. Into the journal went words describing my feelings, my fears and sense of weakness, my hopes, and my discoveries about where Christ was leading me. When I felt empty or defeated, I wrote about that too.
>
> Slowly I began to realize that journaling was helping me come to grips with an enormous part of my inner person that I had never been fully honest about. No longer could fears and struggles remain inside without definition. They were surfaced and named. And I became aware, little by little that God's Holy Spirit was directing many of the thoughts and insights as I wrote. On paper, I felt that God and I were carrying on a personal communion. He was helping me, in the words of David, to "search my heart." He was prodding me to

Transformation Through Journaling

put words to my fears, shapes to my doubts. And when I was candid about it, then there would often come out of Scripture or from the meditations of my own heart the reassurances, the rebukes, and the admonishments that I so badly needed. But this began to happen only when the journal was employed.[1]

A fundamental benefit of journaling is that it motivates you to intentionally withdraw from your hectic daily life and enter the presence of God. It requires you to take stock of your experiences and helps you see them from a new perspective. Making time to think about your life in the context of your relationship with God and your faith will deepen your understanding of your experiences and reactions and help you assimilate how the Lord is working in your life. The journal is a record of our thoughts and spiritual discoveries. It allows us to analyze our experiences from a distance and learn from them instead of just reacting in the moment. This helps clarify our ideas and feelings.

My personal journal has been instrumental in helping me recognize the presence of God in my life. I forget very easily the prayers God has answered and the times in which He has helped me with problems that overwhelmed me. When I review my journal, I realize how present God is, how He cares for me and participates in my life.

For example, in recent years, I suffered from a strange condition that produces horrible vertigo. This condition in my right ear has greatly weakened my health. Finally, I decided to have surgery as a means to get some kind of relief. A few days after my operation, I wrote in my journal the following prayer. Having it written there will allow me to remember for the rest of my life how the Lord was at my side during the most difficult moments of my illness:

Transformation

I Was Never Alone (November 19, 2015)

Just as dawn breaks, I watch the sun's bright journey,
And feel you near, each step along the way.
I ponder, that through life's unceasing battles
I've never felt abandoned, I never felt alone.
The scars I now carry with many of my questions,
I bring to you along with all my praise,
And happily I sing to all who'd listen:
Not even for one second, was I ever left alone.
Just as dawn breaks, I think about my troubles,
The vertigos, the shivering, the fear of a fall,
I wear the scars like badges of your favor,
With humble pride for you, equally dear.
I've pondered of your love, unfailing kindness.
Perplexing mystery! The theme of all my praise.
You've been through all my troubles
Your presence has been constant,
And happily I sing to all who'd listen:
Not even for one second, was I ever left alone.

This prayer will not only serve as a reminder for me but also be a testimony to my children of their father's difficult times and how God strengthened him when he needed it most.

Journaling what you have experienced and learned allows you to become more aware of the presence of God and what He has taught you over time. It also serves as a reminder of the times in which you have been given guidance and when God has acted in your aid and answered or solved complicated situations. Such a record can strengthen your faith, knowing God will do the same in the present and future. Making frequent journal entries and recording our reactions to the experiences

Transformation Through Journaling

we have had can lead to deeper introspection. A journal allows us to observe patterns of behavior that we would otherwise not notice, and the Holy Spirit uses this to provide us with evidence of our growth or to show us where we are sinning. Reviewing what we wrote three, six, or twelve months earlier allows us to analyze more objectively what happened, to more easily identify the objectives achieved and the progress made in a given area so we can decide which aspects we want to concentrate on. A journal can prompt us to make the necessary progress in our relationship with God.

Ellen White kept a personal journal throughout her life. In it, this woman, who dedicated her life to serving God and His church, expresses her pain and doubts. The reality is that, for decades, Ellen suffered a deep spiritual dryness that put her faith to the test. Many times, she wondered whether God would respond. When we think of her life, it's easy to think that she was a human being without spiritual struggles and that she always had all the answers. Nothing is further from reality. In her journal, we can appreciate the struggles and needs and also the victories that all Christians experience in our walk with Christ:

> While bowed at the altar with others who were seeking the Lord, all the language of my heart was: "Help, Jesus; save me, or I perish! I will never cease to entreat till my prayer is heard and my sins are forgiven." I felt my needy, helpless condition as never before.
>
> As I knelt and prayed, suddenly my burden left me, and my heart was light. At first a feeling of alarm came over me, and I tried to resume my load of distress. It seemed to me that I had no right to feel joyous and happy. But Jesus seemed very near to me; I felt able to come to Him with all my griefs, misfortunes, and trials,

Transformation

> even as the needy ones came to Him for relief when He was upon earth. There was a surety in my heart that He understood my peculiar trials, and sympathized with me. I can never forget this precious assurance of the pitying tenderness of Jesus toward one so unworthy of His notice. I learned more of the divine character of Christ in that short period, when bowed among the praying ones, than ever before.[2]

In a journal, you can address the Lord, being honest with Him and with yourself. It serves as a place to confide your fears, frustrations, insecurities, and dislikes and also mark your triumphs, goals, and prayers—the whole spectrum of emotions and thoughts. It is a means of communicating these things to God at the time you are living them and allows you to reconsider situations, if necessary, to reflect on them later and learn. In addition, when you document your spiritual goals and check in with them frequently, you can easily evaluate the progress you are making in those areas. It may serve to remind you of how you have committed to become more like Christ. It can help you feel responsible for prioritizing and achieving your spiritual goals.

Here are a few suggestions for journaling:

- Write from the heart.
- Find a specific time to write daily, such as during your time of daily devotions.
- Reflect on one passage in the Word and write how God can impact your life through the message.
- Write how God is real in your daily life.
- Write on your computer, phone, iPad, or another electronic device.

Transformation Through Journaling

Whatever you decide, just remember that the journals that tend to last are those that are reflected in notebooks and day planners. You may choose to write something every day; others write once a week. There is no rule about how much writing is required. Sometimes, only one sentence confirms the love of God in your life. Your journal is something intimate. Its purpose is to communicate with God in writing and in a safe and private way. The benefits of keeping a journal are achieved by those who persevere.

Reflection

If you kept a journal and periodically reviewed your thoughts and day-to-day life, what would you see? Consistent growth? Or would you realize that your life more often does not reflect what God expects of you?

---

1. Gordon MacDonald, *Ordering Your Private World* (Nashville, TN: W Publishing Group, 2017), 136, 137.
2. Ellen G. White, *Life Sketches of Ellen G. White* (Mountain View, CA: Pacific Press®, 1943), 23, 24.

Chapter 12

Transformation Through Meditation

Another spiritual discipline that will help you develop an intimate relationship with God is meditation. Many have confused this important spiritual discipline with Eastern mystical practices. However, the meditation that the Bible presents as an indispensable instrument in your relationship with God has absolutely nothing to do with the introspective pagan phenomena of concentration or transcendental meditation. Rather, Christian meditation is based on the Bible. In Joshua 1:8, God says that we meditate on His Word by day and by night to obey it.

In the Old Testament, there are two main Hebrew words for meditation: *haga*, which means to utter, moan, meditate, or ponder, and *siakh*, which means to ponder, study, or consider. The following verses use *haga* or *siakh* and instruct us to meditate on the Word of God:

> Keep this Book of the Law always on your lips; meditate on it day and night, so that you may be careful to

Transformation

>do everything written in it. Then you will be prosperous and successful (Joshua 1:8, NIV).

>But his delight is in the law of the LORD,
>And in His law he meditates day and night (Psalm 1:2).

>My soul shall be satisfied as with marrow and fatness,
>And my mouth shall praise You with joyful lips.

>When I remember You on my bed,
>I meditate on You in the night watches.
>Because You have been my help,
>Therefore in the shadow of Your wings I will rejoice (Psalm 63:5–7).

>I will remember the works of the LORD;
>Surely I will remember Your wonders of old.
>I will also meditate on all Your work,
>And talk of Your deeds (Psalm 77:11, 12).

>Your commands are always with me
>>and make me wiser than my enemies.
>I have more insight than all my teachers,
>>for I meditate on your statutes (Psalm 119:98, 99, NIV).

There are three moments in the day when you can actively give your mind to the Word of God in Christian meditation. First, just before bed, you can make the Word of God the last thing that occupies your mind. Second, when you wake up, you can make the Word of God the first thought that fills your mind as you start the day. Finally, you need a specific moment during the day to meditate on the Word of God so it can speak to you at every

Transformation Through Meditation

step and in every decision you make. The best place to begin is the life of Christ. In fact, meditating on Jesus should be your priority:

> It would be well to spend a thoughtful hour each day reviewing the life of Christ from the manger to Calvary. We should take it point by point and let the imagination vividly grasp each scene, especially the closing ones of His earthly life. By thus contemplating His teachings and sufferings, and the infinite sacrifice made by Him for the redemption of the race, we may strengthen our faith, quicken our love, and become more deeply imbued with the spirit which sustained our Saviour. If we would be saved at last we must all learn the lesson of penitence and faith at the foot of the cross. . . . Everything noble and generous in man will respond to the contemplation of Christ upon the cross.[1]

Elsewhere, Ellen G. White describes God's love for you and expresses how meditation on Bible passages can change your relationship with God:

> What love, what matchless love, that, sinners and aliens as we are, we may be brought back to God and adopted into His family! We may address Him by the endearing name, "Our Father," which is a sign of affection for Him and a pledge of His tender regard and relationship to us. . . .
>
> All the paternal love which has come down from generation to generation through the channel of human hearts, all the springs of tenderness which have opened in the souls of men, are but as a tiny rill to the boundless ocean when compared with the infinite,

Transformation

> exhaustless love of God. Tongue cannot utter it; pen cannot portray it. You may meditate upon it every day of your life; you may search the Scriptures diligently in order to understand it; you may summon every power and capability that God has given you, in the endeavor to comprehend the love and compassion of the heavenly Father; and yet there is an infinity beyond. You may study that love for ages; yet you can never fully comprehend the length and the breadth, the depth and the height, of the love of God in giving His Son to die for the world. Eternity itself can never fully reveal it. Yet as we study the Bible and meditate upon the life of Christ and the plan of redemption, these great themes will open to our understanding more and more.[2]

Furthermore, meditation is an excellent tool to use during periods of fasting. While you fast, spend a block of time in prayer, followed by focused Bible study, followed by meditation and reflection on what has been studied and learned. And, when concentration is difficult, remember, "Finally, brothers and sisters, whatever is true, whatever is noble, whatever is right, whatever is pure, whatever is lovely, whatever is admirable—if anything is excellent or praiseworthy—think about such things" (Philippians 4:8, NIV).

Reflection
Consider these words from the Bible: "Examine yourselves to see whether you are in the faith; test yourselves. Do you not realize that Christ Jesus is in you—unless, of course, you fail the test?" (2 Corinthians 13:5, NIV). Outline a plan to examine your faith by combining the use of meditation and fasting in your life.

Transformation Through Meditation

1. Ellen G. White, *Testimonies for the Church*, vol. 4 (Mountain View, CA: Pacific Press®, 1948), 374.

2. Ellen G. White, *Testimonies for the Church*, vol. 5 (Mountain View, CA: Pacific Press®, 1948), 739, 740.

Chapter 13

Transformation Through Stewardship

Stewardship is another spiritual discipline that will help you develop an intimate relationship with God and teach you to trust Him at all times. What, you might ask, is stewardship? It is the way of life of a person who recognizes and accepts the Lordship of Jesus Christ and works in partnership with God, acting as His agent in the administration of His business on Earth. In many ways, stewardship is an outward indication of our inner spiritual growth. "Our attitudes about sharing versus hoarding, giving versus gathering, speak volumes about the condition of our heart and soul. What's more, giving can be a tremendously positive aspect of your relationship, bringing joy and fulfillment as you demonstrate gratitude to God by helping others."[1]

Stewardship originated at creation. All that you can see and touch was created by God. "God created Adam and Eve in His own image and established, with His personal touch, an intimate relationship with humanity."[2] When God created humans, He established them as the stewards of the planet. The Bible states

Transformation

in Genesis 1:26, "Then God said, 'Let us make mankind in our image, in our likeness, so that they may rule over the fish in the sea and the birds in the sky, over the livestock and all the wild animals, and over all the creatures that move along the ground' " (NIV). Christian stewardship is the free and joyful activity of the children of God, through which all life and resources are overseen according to the will of God.

This statement shows that, although God created and sustains of the universe, man was called to administer, or steward, all that belongs to God by right. Maybe you'd be surprised if I told you that you really do not own anything. When you reflect on the reality of life, you realize that one day, you can have everything, and the next, you can lose it all. Governments change, laws are under continuous scrutiny, taxes rise, the stock market is becoming more unstable, your house can succumb to the strong winds of a hurricane or collapse during an earthquake, and you can lose your car in an accident. The security we find in material things is trivial. Anyone can lose their job and deal with the uncertainty of seeking daily sustenance. However, these realities are ignored by many people who remove God from the picture of their lives and selfishly think everything they have is the result of their ability, hard work, and intelligence. Painful error! Taking God out of the equation is not a wise choice. Many do not even consider that everything they have achieved in life is the result of God's blessings.

Every blessing comes from God. However, we live in a world that has told us: "This is your house, your money, your family, your life, your time, your talents; it all belongs to you." Perhaps you believe, and with plenty of reason, that the money you earn as a product of your work is yours and that the things you buy with that money belong to you. However, if you think this way, you are losing sight of an inescapable truth that can forever change the way you look at life. The reality is that everything comes from God, everything belongs to Him, and everything you possess has been placed in your care by God so that you can voluntarily make the decision to manage it for His honor and glory. Understanding this and putting it into practice is a matter of faith. In other words, you need to trust God and put these principles to the test in your life. In fact, there is only one topic in the Bible on which God allows you to test Him. Imagine! The owner of the universe encourages you to put Him to the test. The passage appears in Malachi 3:8–10. Let's analyze the subject.

In this passage, after declaring that His people have robbed Him, God asks His children to learn to trust Him and makes a beautiful promise:

> "Will a mere mortal rob God? Yet you rob me.
>
> "But you ask, 'How are we robbing you?'
>
> "In tithes and offerings. You are under a curse—your whole nation—because you are robbing me. Bring the whole tithe into the storehouse, that there may be food in my house. Test me in this," says the LORD Almighty, "and see if I will not throw open the floodgates of heaven and pour out so much blessing that there will not be room enough to store it" (Malachi 3:8–10, NIV).

God does not impose Himself on us, but He invites us to trust Him. "The Lord does not need our offerings. We cannot enrich him with our gifts. Says the psalmist: 'All things come of thee, and of thine own have we given thee.' Yet God permits us to show our appreciation of his mercies by self-sacrificing efforts to extend the same to others. This is the only way in which it is possible for us to manifest our gratitude and love to God. He

Transformation

has provided no other."[3] Being a good steward is the response of a person who is grateful to God. Good stewardship means acknowledging that everything you have obtained comes from the mercy of God, not as a product of your own effort. In fact, God includes stewardship—the gift of giving and sharing—among the gifts of service given to the church in order to enable her to carry out her ministry in the world (Romans 12:8). The gift of giving has been defined as the ability to earn money and put it along with other possessions in the service of God and the advancement of His kingdom.

Too often, we rely on our ability instead of trusting God to provide for our needs. And the saddest thing is that our heavenly Father does not deserve our lack of faith, mistrust, and rejection. He is good, and He is faithful. Those who have discovered this truth have come to understand what it means to be a good steward of God's resources.

Truly, God blesses those who bless others. Let's think for a moment about this simple statement. You can become an agent of God's blessings. The Word teaches us that God wants His church to fulfill its mission. He blesses you, in part, so that you can support His church. God is never going to abandon the needs of His people. He wants to bless you so that you can be a channel of blessing to others. That's why Jesus said, "Give, and it will be given to you" (Luke 6:38), and "Freely you have received, freely give" (Matthew 10:8). God is always looking to bless His church, His children, and the needy. You can choose to be the channel of blessing or, on the contrary, assuming a selfish attitude, allow God to find another person who becomes that channel of blessing. In the end, God will continue to bless, with or without your support. The church will remain the apple of His eye, and the helpless of the earth, His deepest concern. You can become that faithful steward whom God is seeking for the benefit of His kingdom.

Transformation Through Stewardship

It is important to remember that "none can enter heaven whose characters are defiled by the foul blot of selfishness. Therefore, God tests us here, by committing to us temporal possessions, that our use of these may show whether we can be intrusted with eternal riches."[4]

Hudson Taylor, a missionary in China for many years, understood this mystery of God's faithfulness. He gave the following testimony:

> "Our Father is a very experienced one." . . . "He knows very well that His children wake up with a good appetite every morning, and He always provides breakfast for them, and sees to it also that they do not go to bed supperless at night. . . . He had no difficulty in sustaining two or more millions of Israelites in the wilderness for forty years. We scarcely expect that He will send two million missionaries to China; but if He should do so, He would have abundant means to sustain them all. Let us see to it that we keep God before our eyes, that we walk in His ways, and seek to please and glorify Him in all things great and small. Depend upon it, GOD's work, done in GOD's way, will never lack GOD's supplies.[5]

God does not ask that we give by necessity, that is, by obligation. Many contribute only because there is a need and because they feel compelled to give. God does not ask that we give to satisfy the existing needs. Necessity is not the motive that must impel us to give. Rather, the Christian must respond because his or her life is full of the love of God and that is what God seeks. Consider the following:

Transformation

Honor the LORD with your wealth,
   with the firstfruits of all your crops;
then your barns will be filled to overflowing,
   and your vats will brim over with new wine" (Proverbs 3:9, 10, NIV).

All the good things we have are a loan from our Saviour. He has made us stewards. Our smallest offerings, our humblest services, presented in faith and love, may be consecrated gifts to win souls to the service of the Master and to promote His glory.[6]

Selfishness is the strongest and most general of human impulses, the struggle of the soul between sympathy and covetousness is an unequal contest; for while selfishness is the strongest passion, love and benevolence are too often the weakest, and as a rule the evil gains the victory. Therefore in our labors and gifts for God's cause, it is unsafe to be controlled by feeling or impulse.[7]

When the perfect love of God is in the heart, wonderful things will be done. Christ will be in the heart of the believer as a well of water springing up unto everlasting life. But those who manifest indifference to the suffering ones of humanity will be charged with indifference to Jesus Christ. . . . Those who indulge self and neglect to care for the souls and bodies of those for whom Christ has given his life, are not eating of the bread of life, nor drinking of the water of the well of salvation. They are dry and sapless, like a tree that bears no fruit. They are spiritual dwarfs, who consume

Transformation Through Stewardship

their means on self; but "whatsoever a man soweth, that shall he also reap."[8]

Transformation through stewardship comes by observing these principles:

- God is the owner of everything.
- Giving to God must be our priority.
- God is honored when we give.
- Sharing changes our lives and the lives of others.
- Give without expecting to receive something in return.
- Give joyfully.
- Support the church of God as good stewards.
- Give as a family—parents should teach their children to be generous.

Reflection

Have you ever felt that you have stolen from God? Can God entrust you with His blessings, knowing that you will respond as a good steward of His kingdom?

---

1. Bethany and Scott Palmer, *Cents & Sensibility* (Colorado Springs, CO: David C. Cook, 2005), 218.

2. "Juan E. Gonzales," Southeastern Conference of Seventh-day Adventists, https://www.secsda.org/stewardship/.

3. Ellen G. White, "Our Missions in Europe," *Advent Review and Sabbath Herald*, December 6, 1887, 754.

4. Ellen G. White, "Liberality the Fruit of Love," *Advent Review and Sabbath Herald*, May 16, 1893, 305.

5. M. Geraldine Guinness, *The Story of the China Inland Mission*, vol. 1 (London: Morgan and Scott, 1893), 238.

6. Ellen G. White, *Testimonies for the Church*, vol. 3 (Mountain View, CA: Pacific Press®, 1948), 397.

7. Ellen G. White, "Workers With God," *Advent Review and Sabbath Herald*, December 7, 1886, 753.

8. Ellen G. White, "Followers of Christ Will Be Missionaries," *Advent Review and Sabbath Herald*, January 15, 1895.

Chapter 14

Transformation Through a Spiritual Retreat

Another spiritual discipline that will help you develop an intimate relationship with God and will make you understand your need for rest is the spiritual retreat. We live in a very convoluted world and are often trapped by the maelstrom of constant activities and responsibilities. The hours in a day do not seem to be enough, and sleep often suffers. Stress builds as the realization dawns, *I cannot fulfill all these expectations*. But don't give up! Rather, set aside time to pause and organize your life. Remember, "The richest, happiest and most productive lives are characterized by the ability to fully engage in the challenge at hand, but also to disengage periodically and seek renewal."[1]

We live in a world of constant activity. Advances in technology keep us connected all the time. However, one should ask whether it is precisely this connection that keeps us disconnected from what is really important. I remember hearing someone rightly observe, "Smartphones are here to help us reach out to people who are far away and separate us from the people closest to us."

Transformation

In music, a "rest" is an interval of time when no sound is heard. Silence is necessary to produce good music. Somewhere within the composition, you will find these necessary and important pauses. If you compare your existence to a musical composition, you will realize that in the melody of your life, music is interrupted here and there by those essential "rests." Undoubtedly, all human beings need momentary pauses. It is in these times of silence when the Great Composer is writing the "rests" that can make you grow and teach you the value of what is most important: an intimate relationship with Him.

The reality today is that everyone is tired. It seems clear that addiction to work is a plague in the modern world. However, the Word of God reveals a concept about rest that we should examine. God Himself was the first to "rest." "And He rested on the seventh day from all His work" (Genesis 2:2). "For in six days the LORD made the heavens and the earth, and on the seventh day He rested and was refreshed" (Exodus 31:17). Did God need to rest? Of course not! But He chose to rest. Because God, in His immeasurable wisdom, subjected creation to a rhythm of work and rest. "This rest was not meant to be a luxury but, rather, a necessity for those who wish to grow and mature."[2]

In addition to the observance of the Sabbath, Jesus also intentionally sought occasions to retreat and seek His Father in prayer.

> He seemed as one who was set apart. His hours of happiness were found when alone with nature and with God. Whenever it was His privilege, He turned aside from the scene of His labor, to go into the fields, to meditate in the green valleys, to hold communion with God on the mountainside or amid the trees of the forest. The early morning often found Him in some secluded place, meditating, searching the Scriptures,

Transformation Through a Spiritual Retreat

or in prayer. From these quiet hours He would return to His home to take up His duties again, and to give an example of patient toil.³

These retreats helped Him stay in an intimate relationship with God. Jesus retired to a separate place to communicate with His Father and rest. There, He was often found by His disciples. Several times, the Gospels refer to the multitudes seeking Him and finding Him in a deserted place. In fact, the feeding of the five thousand occurs because Christ was found resting in a secluded place. But before His public ministry began, He spent time in solitude in the desert. During this time, He fought His first great battle in favor of human beings. The Bible says that it was there, in that retreat, that Satan tempted Him fiercely. Everything was at stake, but the results of that first spiritual retreat prepared the Master for His ministry. It was the basis of the other great victories that would take Him through the difficult moments to Golgotha.

The Bible records several instances of Jesus spending time alone with the Father: "One of those days Jesus went out to a mountainside to pray, and spent the night praying to God. When morning came, he called his disciples to him and chose twelve of them, whom he also designated apostles" (Luke 6:12, 13, NIV).

"Very early in the morning, while it was still dark, Jesus got up, left the house and went off to a solitary place, where he prayed" (Mark 1:35, NIV).

"At daybreak, Jesus went out to a solitary place. The people were looking for him and when they came to where he was, they tried to keep him from leaving them" (Luke 4:42, NIV).

"Then, because so many people were coming and going that they did not even have a chance to eat, he said to them, 'Come with me by yourselves to a quiet place and get some rest' " (Mark 6:31, NIV).

Transformation

Regarding Jesus' forty days in the wilderness before beginning His ministry, the Spirit of Prophecy comments, "He went to the wilderness to be alone, to contemplate His mission and work. By fasting and prayer He was to brace Himself for the bloodstained path He must travel."[4]

And concerning Jesus' invitation to the apostles, "Come aside by yourselves to a deserted place and rest a while" (Mark 6:31), we read, "Near Bethsaida, at the northern end of the lake, was a lonely region, now beautiful with the fresh green of spring, that offered a welcome retreat to Jesus and His disciples. For this place they set out, going in their boat across the water. Here they would be away from the thoroughfares of travel, and the bustle and agitation of the city. The scenes of nature were in themselves a rest, a change grateful to the senses."[5]

Consider the following recommendations that can greatly help you in your physical and spiritual renewal:

- *Take a vacation regularly.* In today's world, our society does not take enough time to disconnect. Many people are slaves of "duty." However, when scheduling vacations, do not use the time to catch up on things that you are behind in or to do more work.
- *Intentionally separate time for spiritual retreats.* I recommend setting aside half to a full day for a retreat each month. During these times, have no agenda. Just listen to the voice of God through prayer and His Word.
- *Make time to connect with God daily.* Take the opportunity to seek God in prayer and in His Word. Seek God as a child seeks the protection of his father. Never make important decisions without seeking God's will. Get out of the office, stop your work for a few minutes, and walk around the neighborhood for a while. Remember, "From

hours spent with God He came forth morning by morning, to bring the light of heaven to men. Daily He received a fresh baptism of the Holy Spirit. In the early hours of the new day the Lord awakened Him from His slumbers, and His soul and His lips were anointed with grace, that He might impart to others."[6]

- Enjoy the Sabbath. Take the Sabbath seriously and rest from the stress of work. Enter the hours of the Sabbath with a spirit of renewal and adoration. Sabbath must be a delight, never a burden.
- Engage in recreational activities. Find time for fun by engaging in activities that get you out of the rut and stress of work. Understand that you are more than a work machine, and as a human being, you need to devote time to recreation.

In short, transformation through a spiritual retreat is possible only when we resist the natural tendency to fill our lives with work and activities. Learn to delegate. Go to bed early. Read a psalm and plan or evaluate your day. Start the day with a devotional. Plan to spend a few minutes in prayer throughout the day. Organize your time so you have periodic times to pray or rest.

Reflection

Do you schedule a time to rest so you can renew yourself in body, soul, and spirit like Jesus did? If not, make a plan to do so soon.

---

1. Jim Loehr and Tony Schwartz, *The Power of Full Engagement* (New York: The Free Press, 2005), 12.
2. Gordon MacDonald, *Ordering Your Private World* (Nashville, TN: W Publishing Group, 2017), 176.
3. Ellen G. White, *The Desire of Ages* (Nampa, ID: Pacific Press®, 2005), 89, 90.
4. White, 114.
5. White, 361.
6. Ellen G. White, *Christ's Object Lessons* (Washington, DC: Review and Herald®, 1969), 139.

Appendix

Spiritual Inventory

To carry out this spiritual inventory, it is recommended that you plan on at least eight hours for completion. It would be an ideal activity to incorporate with a spiritual retreat. As you go through the exercise, you will better understand why a transformation in your life is so important. Some questions might seem difficult to answer, but they really aren't; you want to avoid them because they expose your reality. If you prefer not to answer them, continue with the retreat, and you can always return to the question(s) when the Spirit moves you to.

Are you ready? I wish you a beautiful day with God, and may the Holy Spirit guide you through this spiritual journey. Above all, I wish that at the end of the retreat, you find yourself truly transformed.

In search of His presence
Many times, you are busy with daily activities, and you lose sight of what should be a priority in your life. The story of Martha and

Transformation

Mary speaks of a similar experience:

> As Jesus and his disciples were on their way, he came to a village where a woman named Martha opened her home to him. She had a sister called Mary, who sat at the Lord's feet listening to what he said. But Martha was distracted by all the preparations that had to be made. She came to him and asked, "Lord, don't you care that my sister has left me to do the work by myself? Tell her to help me!"
>
> "Martha, Martha," the Lord answered, "you are worried and upset about many things, but few things are needed—or indeed only one. Mary has chosen what is better, and it will not be taken away from her" (Luke 10:38–42, NIV).

Ask yourself: Am I sitting at the feet of Jesus, or do I find myself busy doing many other things? Jesus' response to Martha is interesting: "Mary has chosen what is better." What Martha was doing was necessary; someone had to prepare food for Jesus and His disciples. However, Jesus said that the most important thing was beyond the pursuits of this life, and in this case, the priority of the moment was to be in His presence. The purpose of a spiritual retreat is to sit at the feet of Jesus to recharge your spiritual batteries. Take time to

- reflect and evaluate your walk with Jesus in the past,
- reflect and evaluate your walk with Jesus in the present,
- be guided by the Holy Spirit to do only the will of God in your life,
- cultivate intimacy with God, and
- foster fellowship with other disciples.

Spiritual Inventory

What should you bring to the retreat?

- a positive attitude
- a humble spirit
- pencil or pen for writing
- notebook
- a watch
- Bible
- prayer list

To begin

One thing that keeps your devotional life from producing a close relationship with God is not having a plan of action or discipline that allows you to be consistent. It is interesting to note that you value the importance of having a plan of action for your home, professional, and academic lives, but you do not have a plan of action for your devotional life with Jesus. Many times, you mark the calendar with important appointments, but you do not mark the appointments of love and intimacy that you must have with Jesus daily. You have many important activities and give them the necessary importance, but devotional time with God sadly ends up being pushed to the background.

The first thing you have to do to have a fruitful devotional life is to intentionally set aside daily time for your communion with Jesus. In the same way that you have separated these hours for this spiritual retreat, you must set aside some time each day to have a "love date" with Jesus.

Secondly, define a specific place where you will seek God daily. The success of a devotional plan lies in having a place reserved for this special activity. This does not mean you cannot talk to God elsewhere, but this place is where you have your appointment with the Eternal One. God hears your prayer wherever you are,

Transformation

but having a special place signals you are intentional in your meeting with Him. Companionship is always marked by meeting places where intimate moments are shared between two people who love each other.

Third, you need to put some thought into the structure of your time with God. What will be the main components of that time? When you want to know someone intimately, you take time to listen, and then you talk with that person. You tell other people about the relationship you have built. The same is true of Jesus. You must listen, speak, and share Jesus with others.

In this spiritual retreat, you will divide time into three parts:

1. Meditate, read, and listen to the Word. In this section, you will meditate on the presence of God in your past and present.

2. Talk to God. In this section you will speak with God, presenting your petitions and the requests of others before Him.

3. Share with others the experience you have had with God, the presence of God in your past. After all, "we have nothing to fear for the future, except as we shall forget the way the Lord has led us, and His teaching in our past history."[1]

Digging into the Word
1. *Read the Word.* Prayerfully read and meditate on Isaiah 49:1–7; Proverbs 3:5, 6; and Jeremiah 1:4–9.

2. *Interpret the Word.* What are the main points you find in these texts? (Invest enough time in this exercise).

3. *Apply the Word.* As you meditate on your past, consider how many thoughts and memories come to mind about God's provision, care, and love for you?

Spiritual Inventory

Steps to analyze your life
1. Think about the different stages of your life. Look for transitional events or decisive or crucial moments. Make a list of crucial or decisive events that have impacted your spiritual life:

2. Select one of these decisive or crucial events that was significant in your life. Write it, then describe the situation. What did you learn? Finally, mention what you perceived as the role of God in that crucial event and what you learned from that experience with God.

- Crucial or decisive event:

- Describe the situation:

- What did you learn?

- How did you interpret God's role at this crucial point?

- How does this event illustrate what the verses studied said about the presence of God in your life?

Presence of God in your present and future
Read and reflect on the following quote:

> If we keep the Lord ever before us, allowing our hearts to go out in thanksgiving and praise to Him, we shall have a continual freshness in our religious life. Our prayers will take the form of a conversation with God as we would talk with a friend. He will speak His mysteries to us personally. Often there will come to us a sweet joyful sense of the presence of Jesus. Often

Transformation

our hearts will burn within us as He draws nigh to commune with us as He did with Enoch. When this is in truth the experience of the Christian, there is seen in His life a simplicity, a humility, meekness, and lowliness of heart, that show to all with whom he associates that he has been with Jesus and learned of Him."[2]

- How is God making His presence known in your life today?

- As you consider the future, what promises does the Holy Spirit bring to mind?

Meditating on the Bible
1. *Read the Word.* John 15:1–17; 1 Timothy 4:9–16.
Pray with an open heart, mind, and soul while doing an unhurried and reflective reading of the Word of God.

2. *Interpret the Word.* John 15:1–17.
- How does the metaphor of the vine and the branches describe the relationship Christ wants to have with you?

- What does it mean to remain (dwell, live, or abide) in Christ?

- What is the function of God the Father?

- What is the relationship between bearing fruit and remaining in Christ?

- What is the relationship between bearing fruit and an answered prayer?

Spiritual Inventory

- What do verses 9–12 tell you about human relationships?

- What did Jesus say is the characteristic of a true disciple?

- What does verse 16 tell you about your future ministry?

3. Interpretation of the Word—1 Timothy 4:9–16.
   - Do you find encouragement in these words?

   - Which of the instructions Paul gives Timothy is best applied to your life?

   - How can you use this passage to define your ministry in the church?

4. *Apply the Word*. Write three things you think God would like to improve in your spiritual life this year. Allow yourself to dream of what could happen through the power of God in your life.

Answer the following questions:
   a. What can I do to improve my relationship with Christ?

   b. What can I do to improve my relationships with others (my spouse, child, parent, friend, enemy, etc.)?

   c. What can I do to ensure that my ministry gives glory to God alone?

5. Meditate on what you would like God to do in your future. Claim the Bible promises you have studied. Do not worry about human motivations; God can help you deal with them later. Allow

Transformation

yourself to dream of what could happen in your life through the power of God. Write your dreams and plans for the future.

6. Pray and ask God to purify your motives, empower you to follow His will, and glorify His name through your life. Remember, "Do not neglect secret prayer, for it is the soul of religion. With earnest, fervent prayer, plead for purity of soul. Plead as earnestly, as eagerly, as you would for your mortal life, were it at stake. Remain before God until unutterable longings are begotten within you for salvation, and the sweet evidence is obtained of pardoned sin."[3]

In intimacy with the Eternal One
Cry out to God on behalf of your relationship with Him and others. Remember that "prayer is the breath of the soul. It is the secret of spiritual power. No other means of grace can be substituted, and the health of the soul preserved. Prayer brings the heart into immediate contact with the Well-spring of life, and strengthens the sinew and muscle of religious experience. Neglect the exercise of prayer, or engage in prayer spasmodically, now and then, as seems convenient, and you lose your hold on God."[4]

1. Make a list of people you want to bring to the Lord or encourage in their walk with Him this year and cry out to God for each of those names.

2. Write a list of concerns, and pray over them.

> a. Think about conflicts, problems, concerns, or frustrations and write them down. Any concerns you have should be on this list.

b. Go through the list, one by one. With each written problem, determine whether you can do something to solve it. It may be that the situation is beyond your control, or maybe you can do something about it.

c. Whatever your conclusion, pray for each written matter. But if you think you can take action on a particular issue, write what the Spirit of God shows you to do in regard to that concern. You may find other things to add to the list through this sincere season of prayer. Be sure to write them down and think about possible solutions.

Prayer and promise

Next, you will study eight texts. Each contains a verse of prayer or promise. Read the text, write it down, meditate on it with prayer, and then record your response to the promise of God in the white space.

1. *Salvation*. Psalm 138:7, 8
My response:

2. *Peace*. Jeremiah 29:11–14
My response:

3. *Joy*. Philippians 4:4–6
My response:

4. *Strength*. Ephesians 3:16
My response:

Transformation

5. *Effort and courage.* Joshua 1:6, 7
My response:

6. *A clean heart.* Psalm 51:10–12
My response:

7. *Wisdom.* Colossians 1:9–14
My response:

8. *Praise.* Psalm 103:1–5
My response:

Reflection
- Is there anything in your life (a habit, attitude, desire, etc.) that is negatively affecting your relationship with God?

- What are some changes you must make in your life to be more intentional in spiritual growth and in your relationship with Christ?

- Are there areas in your life where you are playing with sin? What must you do to remove these temptations?

- Is there anyone in your life who has offended you and you have not forgiven? What would it take for you to forgive him/her?

- In what areas of your life have you most obviously seen

Spiritual Inventory

the hand of God? What are you doing to nourish that area of your life?

- If you feel comfortable, share with someone you trust what you have written and ask for their support and prayer.

Spiritual maturity and true transformation
To meditate, consider the following questions:
- Do you think Jesus would recognize you as His disciple?
- Does your life reflect that Jesus is the center of your existence?
- Do your thoughts express that you love your Lord and Savior?
- Has your life really changed direction?
- Who are you really?
- Write how the power of God has manifested itself in your life, bringing out the best in you and transforming you through His Spirit to become more like Jesus.

The Holy Spirit helps you find the answers
1. Conviction
What does God want to change in your life today?

Are you allowing the Holy Spirit to show you what you must do to reach lost souls?

2. Conversion
Are you assured that God loves you?

Have you received forgiveness and become a new person?

Transformation

3. Bible study
Are you spending significant time with God through the study of His Word?

4. Christian character
How do you need to be more like Jesus in character?

What sins and temptations do you need to overcome through the power of God in your life?

5. Prayer
Are you bringing your problems to God in prayer and surrendering your life to Jesus every day?

Are you praying for the lost?

6. Good works
Are you helping others in the same way Christ did?

In what areas can you grow so you can help others more effectively?

7. Testimony
Are you bearing witness that you are a disciple of Christ?

Can those around you see Christ in your life?

8. Community of believers
Do you love others as Christ loves you, helping, understanding, and forgiving them?

Do you regularly meet with other Christians to pray, study the Bible, and encourage each other?

Spiritual Inventory

9. Worship
Do you feel the continued presence of God in your life?

Do you feel the presence of God in your congregation? Is Sabbath a blessing for your life because you spend it in God's company?

10. Multiplication
Are you praying daily for the outpouring of the Holy Spirit?

Are you encouraging your congregation to be faithful to the Lord with resources, time, and talents?

The seven questions of spiritual growth
Evaluate from 1–10 (1 being the least, and 10 being the most)

_____ 1. Your trust and faith in God in all things
_____ 2. Your life in light of the responsibility to testify, in actions, not words
_____ 3. Your life in the area of trusting in God
_____ 4. Your life as an instrument of God's power
_____ 5. Your level of freedom from worries, anxiety, and fear
_____ 6. The level of mercy and compassion for those who live in pain and suffer injustice
_____ 7. Your commitment to participation in the service of the church of Christ

Your worldview
A worldview is based on concepts and structures that guide your outlook on the world. From it originate your opinions, beliefs, attitudes, and actions. Some of these life tenets may help in the spiritual growth of the Christian, but many have a negative effect on spiritual development of the believer. Consider the following:

Transformation

A perspective or rule of life that is generally accepted by the majority can become stagnant. This is neither spontaneous nor inspired by the Spirit; therefore, it is not grounded in truth and becomes formal and legalistic.

The maturity of the Christian is an act of balance between opposing factors:

1. structure and freedom
2. the law and the Spirit
3. doctrine and spirituality
4. *gnōsis* (knowledge) and *ginōskō* (relationship)
5. love for the things of the world and life in the context of eternity
6. the tension between faith and unbelief

Plan of action:
1. What is your perspective on reality or life tenet? Where are your priorities?

2. Can you think of an incident in your life when your actions or reactions showed an atheistic or secular behavior instead of a Christlike response?

3. Think of an incident in your life when you showed full confidence in God and He led you as a true disciple of Christ.

4. What can you do to live steadily under the influence of the Holy Spirit and with a Christian perspective?

Remember, this inventory will not fulfill its purpose unless you are totally transparent and honest in answering these questions in the light of God's Word. As these passages and questions point

Spiritual Inventory

you to areas of sin, confess, repent, and renew your commitment to Christ. If you complete this spiritual inventory thoughtfully and prayerfully, you should be able to better understand the will of God for your life.

1. Am I sure that I have eternal life? (1 John 5:13)
   ____Yes ____No
2. Do I trust in Christ alone for my salvation? (Ephesians 2:8, 9)
   ____Yes ____No
3. Is God pleased with my priorities? (Matthew 6:33)
   ____Yes ____No
4. Do I have a biblical purpose for my life? (Philippians 1:20, 21)
   ____Yes ____No
5. Do I have a growing relationship with Christ? (Colossians 2:6, 7)
   ____Yes ____No
6. Does the Word of God give me joy? (Jeremiah 15:16)
   ____Yes ____No
7. Is my life fruitful? (John 15:16)
   ____Yes ____No
8. Am I filled with the Holy Spirit daily? (Ephesians 5:18–20)
   ____Yes ____No
9. Am I willing to learn? (Proverbs 18:15)
   ____Yes ____No
10. Do I encourage my friends to correct me? (Proverbs 9:8, 27:17)
    ____Yes ____No
11. Do I have the attitude of a servant? (Matthew 20:28)
    ____Yes ____No
12. Can I forgive? (Matthew 6:14, 15)
    ____Yes ____No
13. Do I have any roots of bitterness in my heart? (Hebrews 12:15)
    ____Yes ____No
14. Is God content with my thoughts? (Philippians 4:8, 9)
    ____Yes ____No

Transformation

15. Do I accept myself? (Psalm 139:14)

    ____Yes ____No

16. Do I have a clear conscience? (Acts 24:16)

    ____Yes ____No

17. Do I live at peace with myself and others? (Ephesians 4:31, 32)

    ____Yes ____No

18. Do I really hate sin? (Psalm 119:104)

    ____Yes ____No

19. Am I susceptible to anger? (1 Corinthians 13:5)

    ____Yes ____No

20. Do I please God in my prayer life? (Philippians 4:6)

    ____Yes ____No

---

1. Ellen G. White, *Life Sketches of Ellen G. White* (Mountain View, CA: Pacific Press®, 1943), 196.

2. Ellen G. White, *Christ's Object Lessons* (Washington, DC: Review and Herald®, 1969), 129, 130.

3. Ellen G. White, *Testimonies for the Church,* vol. 1 (Mountain View, CA: Pacific Press®, 1948), 163.

4. Ellen G. White, *Gospel Workers* (Washington, DC: Review and Herald®, 1915), 254, 255.